God, Evil, and Suffering in Islam

In this volume, Salih Sayilgan explores the problem of evil and suffering in Islamic theology along with the questions that both religious and nonreligious people alike perennially ask: Why is there evil and suffering? What is God's role in both natural and moral evil? If God is loving, just, and powerful, why is there innocent suffering? Do humans have free will or are they predestined to act in a certain way? Examining both theoretical and practical theodicy in Islam, Sayilgan provides Muslim perspectives on natural and moral evil in light of Islamic theological concepts. He interrogates several specific topics related to evil and suffering, including death, sickness, aging, disability, climate change, and pandemics. These topics are explored through case studies from the lives of Muslims, with particular attention given to the American context. A comparative and dialogical study, this volume also engages with Zoroastrian, Hindu, Buddhist, Jewish, and Christian approaches, as well as nonreligious perspectives.

This title is part of the Flip it Open Programme and may also be available Open Access. Check our website Cambridge Core for details.

SALIH SAYILGAN is an assistant teaching professor in the Department of Theology and Religious Studies at Georgetown University. He is the author of *Exploring Islam: Theology and Spiritual Practice in America* (Fortress Press, 2021).

SALIH SAYILGAN
Georgetown University

God, Evil, and Suffering in Islam

Shaftesbury Road, Cambridge CB2 8EA, United Kingdom

One Liberty Plaza, 20th Floor, New York, NY 10006, USA

477 Williamstown Road, Port Melbourne, VIC 3207, Australia

314–321, 3rd Floor, Plot 3, Splendor Forum, Jasola District Centre, New Delhi – 110025, India

103 Penang Road, #05–06/07, Visioncrest Commercial, Singapore 238467

Cambridge University Press is part of Cambridge University Press & Assessment, a department of the University of Cambridge.

We share the University's mission to contribute to society through the pursuit of education, learning and research at the highest international levels of excellence.

www.cambridge.org
Information on this title: www.cambridge.org/9781009377317

DOI: 10.1017/9781009377294

© Salih Sayilgan 2024

This work is in copyright. It is subject to statutory exceptions and to the provisions of relevant licensing agreements; with the exception of the Creative Commons version the link for which is provided below, no reproduction of any part of this work may take place without the written permission of Cambridge University Press.

An online version of this work is published at doi.org/10.1017/9781009377294 under a Creative Commons Open Access license CC-BY-NC-ND 4.0 which permits re-use, distribution and reproduction in any medium for non-commercial purposes providing appropriate credit to the original work is given. You may not distribute derivative works without permission. To view a copy of this license, visit https://creativecommons.org/licenses/by-nc-nd/4.0

All versions of this work may contain content reproduced under license from third parties. Permission to reproduce this third-party content must be obtained from these third-parties directly. When citing this work, please include a reference to the DOI 10.1017/9781009377294

First published 2024

A catalogue record for this publication is available from the British Library

Library of Congress Cataloging-in-Publication Data
NAMES: Sayilgan, Salih, author.
TITLE: God, evil, and suffering in Islam / Salih Sayilgan.
DESCRIPTION: 1. | New York : Cambridge University Press, 2024. | Includes bibliographical references and index.
IDENTIFIERS: LCCN 2023030695 | ISBN 9781009377317 (hardback) | ISBN 9781009377294 (ebook)
SUBJECTS: LCSH: Good and evil – Religious aspects – Islam. | Suffering – Religious aspects – Islam. | God (Islam)
CLASSIFICATION: LCC BP188 .S335 2024 | DDC 297.2–dc23/eng/20230712
LC record available at https://lccn.loc.gov/2023030695

ISBN 978-1-009-37731-7 Hardback

Cambridge University Press & Assessment has no responsibility for the persistence or accuracy of URLs for external or third-party internet websites referred to in this publication and does not guarantee that any content on such websites is, or will remain, accurate or appropriate.

Dedicated to the memory of Meryem

Everything will perish except His Face. Judgment belongs to Him, and to Him you will be returned.

Qur'an 28:88

I complain of my sorrow and grief to God alone.

Qur'an 12:86

Contents

Acknowledgments		*page* ix
Introduction		1
PART I GOD AND THE PROBLEM OF EVIL		
1	Mapping the Problem	13
2	God, Angels, Humans, and Satan	35
3	Natural Evil and the Role of God	55
4	Moral Evil, Freedom, and Predestination	76
PART II HUMAN NATURE AND SUFFERING		
5	Aging, Loneliness, and Filial Piety	97
6	Illness and Healing	112
7	Death, Resurrection, and the Hereafter	125
PART III CONTEMPORARY QUESTIONS		
8	Disability, the Blind, and God's Justice	143
9	The Environment and Climate Change	157

CONTENTS

10	**Plagues, Pandemics, and Coronavirus**	171
	Conclusion	183
	Bibliography	188
	Index	200

Acknowledgments

There are many people who helped me on the journey of writing this book. I am thankful to Kim Harnes and Megan Grande, who read the first draft of the manuscript. Their suggestions improved the text considerably and saved me from many errors. I am warmly indebted to Alparslan Acikgenç, Osamah Saleh, Said Özervarlı, and Mustafa Uluçay, who guided me to the right resources in the field and revised some of the translations from Turkish and Arabic.

The problem of evil and suffering has often been part of the conversations with my colleagues in the Department of Theology and Religious Studies at Georgetown University. The exchanges have deepened my understanding of the matter. I am especially grateful to Paul Heck, Annalisa Butticci, Matthew Anderson, Frederick Ruf, Min-Ah Cho, Peter Phan, Lauve H. Steenhuisen, Kerry Danner, Leo Lefebure, and Lisa Zaina. I am also thankful to Ariel Glucklich, Julia Lamm, Alan C. Mitchell, Erin Cline, Stephen M. Wilson, Jonathan Ray, and William Werpehowski for their collegiality and support.

My students at Georgetown University read the draft of some of the chapters of this book. Their questions and comments shaped this study. I have also been teaching for Georgetown's Prison and Justice Initiative. As part of this program, I have taught one of my courses at a prison facility in Maryland. My inmate students also read a few chapters. The perspectives of the incarcerated community on the topic enriched my thinking immensely. Many aspects of this work would be incomplete without the contribution of my students. I am thankful to all of them.

ACKNOWLEDGMENTS

I have been attending a family Qur'an study group for a number of years now. The problem of evil and suffering has been a recurring theme of our discussions. The gathering is intergenerational and includes participants from all walks of life. To the Waheed, Shikoh, Munir, Siddiqui, Awan, Puthawala, and Sheikh families, I am grateful for your insights from the Qur'an.

I owe a special thanks to Beatrice Rehl and her team at Cambridge University Press. Beatrice supported this project from the beginning and always addressed my questions and concerns with patience and generosity. I am also indebted to the two anonymous readers for their thoughtful and constructive reviews.

My heartfelt gratitude goes to my family for their love and care while I was working on this project. My wife, Zeyneb, also a scholar in Islamic studies, remains a helpful critic of my work and I treasure our many daily conversations on the question of evil and suffering.

x

Introduction

On the first day of 2022, a tragic story made its way to the major news headlines and went viral on social media. The report was about an Afghan woman who froze to death near the village of Belasur in Iran across from Turkey's Van province. Escaping the Taliban regime, she was attempting to enter Turkey to seek asylum along with her two children, whose ages were eight and nine. Because of the mother's sacrifice, the children survived the freezing cold. When they were found, their hands were covered with their mother's socks, and the mother's feet were covered with plastic bags.[1]

There are many questions that one can raise in the context of God, evil, and suffering in light of this story. The compassion of a mother toward her children is known to be the manifestation of God's mercy in Islamic theology. If the mother was able to sacrifice herself, why did God not do anything to reveal his benevolence and stop this tragedy? If God is omnipotent, why did he not use his power to save the mother of these two innocent children? If God is omniscient, why did he not use his knowledge to make space for a safe journey for them? These are questions that can be raised by religious and nonreligious people.

According to a survey that included the question "if you could ask God only one question and you knew he would give you an answer, what would you ask?" the most common response was

---

[1] "Afghan Woman Freezes to Death near Turkey-Iran Border," *Hurriyet Daily News*, January 2, 2022, www.hurriyetdailynews.com/afghan-woman-freezes-to-death-near-turkey-iran-border-170522.

INTRODUCTION

"why is there pain and suffering in the world?"[2] Probably there is no one issue that is more challenging to religion in general and to the idea of a theistic God in particular than the problem of evil and suffering. The challenge is often known as the "rock of atheism." There are a number of reasons for this objection. Here I mention some of them. First, many atheists believe that suffering that exists in the world is one of the strongest arguments against the existence of God as described in the Abrahamic religions. Even if the reality of evil does not disprove God, it questions the depiction of God as powerful and compassionate. Bart D. Ehrman, who was raised as a believer in God and became a prominent scholar of religion in the United States, lost his faith because of this problem:

> If there is an all-powerful and loving God in this world, why is there so much excruciating pain and unspeakable suffering? The problem of suffering has haunted me for a very long time. It was what made me begin to think about religion when I was young, and it was what led me to question my faith when I was older. Ultimately, it was the reason I lost my faith.[3]

A similar approach comes from Jeffry R. Halverson, a professor of Islamic studies and history of religions at Coastal Carolina University. Halverson became Muslim during his college years. After ten years of his conversion, he left Islam because of the problem of evil and suffering and provides the following reasoning:

> It was the problem of evil and innocent suffering that truly led me out of Islam, and most important, out of religion as a whole. In all of my studies of religious texts and the wonderfully intricate and sophisticated theologies articulated by great Muslim scholars, such as al-Juwayni, al-Ghazali or al-Qushayri, I could not find a satisfying

[2] James R. Beebe, "Logical Problem of Evil," *Internet Encyclopedia of Philosophy*, accessed January 4, 2022, www.iep.utm.edu/evil-log/#H1.

[3] Bart D. Ehrman, *God's Problem: How the Bible Fails to Answer Our Most Important Question – Why We Suffer* (New York: HarperOne, 2009), 1.

INTRODUCTION

explanation for the horrific innocent suffering we see again and again in our world.[4]

Second, many atheists and agnostics have indicated that religion is the source of many atrocities in the world. Absolute truth claims, exclusive views about other religions, unconditional obedience to religious doctrines and their interpretations, and the use of religion for politics, including waging wars, have made religion a source of evil in many parts of the world. Critics also say that religion is an obstacle to critical thinking and moral progress. Not to mention that there is so much violence in the name of religion. It often promotes intolerance and divisions. In 2006, *The Root of All Evil*, a television documentary, was broadcasted on Channel 4 in the United Kingdom. It was written and presented by Richard Dawkins. Dawkins believes that religion is bad for human society and is the root cause of much evil. He supports his points with more details in his book *The God Delusion*. Inspired by John Lennon's (d. 1980) song "Imagine," Dawkins invites his readers to imagine a world with no religion:

> Imagine no suicide bombers, no 9/11, no 7/7, no crusades, no witch-hunts, no Gunpowder plot, no Indian partition, no Israeli/Palestinian wars, no Serb/Croat/Muslim massacres, no persecution of Jews as "Christ-killers," no Northern Ireland "troubles," no "honor killings," no shiny-suited bouffant-haired televangelists fleecing gullible people of their money ("God wants you to give till it hurts"). Imagine no Taliban to blow up ancient statues, no public beheadings of blasphemers, no flogging of female skin for the crime of showing an inch of it.[5]

Again, Dawkins's main thesis is that our world would be better without religion.

---

[4] Jeffry R. Halverson, "I Left Both Christianity and Islam Behind," *Salon*, January 5, 2022, www.salon.com/2015/08/29/i_left_both_christianity_and_islam_behind_it_was_the_problem_of_evil_and_innocent_suffering_that_truly_led_me_out_of_religion/.

[5] Richard Dawkins, preface to *The God Delusion* (New York: Mariner Books, 2008), 23–24.

3

INTRODUCTION

Third, atheists often argue that people believe in religion because of the problem of evil. Generally speaking, our world is a cruel place that makes people vulnerable and frightened. In a world where there is so much evil and suffering, people turn to religion for comfort. Fear is the foundation of religion. Bertrand Russell (d. 1970) pointed to this aspect of faith:

> Religion is based, I think, primarily and mainly upon fear. It is partly the terror of the unknown, and partly, as I have said, the wish to feel that you have a kind of elder brother who will stand by you in all your troubles and disputes. Fear is the basis of the whole thing – fear of the mysterious, fear of defeat, fear of death. Fear is the parent of cruelty, and therefore it is no wonder if cruelty and religion has gone hand-in-hand.[6]

For example, a person who has lost a loved one to death or has a fear of death may find consolation in the idea of the afterlife and heaven. A person who has a chronic illness may find hope in the religious teachings of reward in the hereafter because of their illness. Instead of fearlessly facing and accepting the reality of pain and adversity in the world, people seek support from a supernatural being.

The problem of evil and suffering is not only a question for atheists but also an issue for people who are religious. Faith traditions including Islam cannot be indifferent to this subject. In this regard, Muslim scholars are faced with many questions: Why is there evil and suffering? What is God's role in both natural and moral evil? What is the fate of Muslims who commit moral evil and cause suffering not only to their fellow human beings but also to the natural world? What is the status of a mortal sinner? If God is just, why is there innocent suffering? Do humans have free will or are they predestined to act in a certain way? If God is all-knowing and all-powerful, why is there still accountability in the hereafter, given that he already knows what humans will do?

---

[6] Bertrand Russell, *Why I Am Not a Christian: And Other Essays on Religion and Related Subjects* (New York: Simon & Schuster, 1953), 22.

INTRODUCTION

The existence of evil and suffering is used as evidence for the existence of God and the hereafter as well as the significance of religion in Islamic theology. First, unlike atheists' arguments, mercy, compassion, and solidary infuse the world. This is explained as the manifestation of God's names: the most merciful, the most compassionate, the most generous, and so on. The Qur'an points to this aspect as follows: "You will not see any imperfection in the creation of the Most Merciful. So turn your vision again! Do you see any flaw?"[7] For example, the care and compassion of mothers toward their children is the manifestation of this name of God. Second, in the face of the evil and suffering that exist in the world, Islam teaches its followers to be charitable, forgiving, and compassionate and to stand for justice. Third, for unresolved injustices, unfilled desires, and attachments, it teaches that there is the hereafter and accountability. God's justice will be fully revealed, and those who cause suffering will be held accountable while the innocents will be compensated with eternal bliss for their grief. They find hope through belief in the hereafter.

From an Islamic theological perspective, people's attraction to religion is not about their fear of evil in the world. In the face of pain, cruelty, and suffering, relying on a higher being and longing for eternity is part of human nature. Here I provide two cases. One of them is the story of Hamza Yusuf Hanson, who became one of the most public faces of Islam in America. Hanson turned to Islam after a near-death experience in a car accident. This unexpected confrontation with his mortality led him to do research on religions

---

[7] Qur'an 67:3. For the references from the Qur'an, I offer my own translation. I also consulted the following: Yusuf Ali, *The Meaning of the Holy Qur'an* (Beltsville, MD: Amana, 2003); M. A. S. Abdel Haleem, *The Qur'an: English Translation and Parallel Arabic Text* (Oxford: Oxford University Press, 2010); Majid Fakhry, *An Interpretation of the Qur'an: English Translation of the Meanings* (New York: New York University Press, 2004); Seyyed Hossein Nasr et al., *The Study Quran: A New Translation and Commentary* (New York: HarperOne, 2015); and Marmaduke Pickthall, *The Meaning of the Glorious Qur'an* (New York: Everyman's Library, 1992).

INTRODUCTION

and the hereafter. He found comfort in the vivid details of Islamic eschatology.[8] Another example is Yusuf Islam (better known as Cat Stevens). At the peak of his career, he also had a near-death experience. While swimming in the Pacific Ocean off the coast of Malibu, Islam found himself on the verge of drowning. He describes this incident as follows: "I decided to turn back and head for shore and, of course, at that point I realized, 'I'm fighting the Pacific.' There was no way I was going to win. There was only one thing to do and that was to pray to the almighty to save me. And I did."[9] Islam points out that his prayer to God saved him, and he was able to return to land.

As part of my teaching work at my current institution, I offer a course on the problem of evil and suffering. The student body is very diverse. In a way, it reflects the religious diversity in America. A quarter of my students are usually atheist or agnostic. I then have students from many religious backgrounds, including Hindus, Buddhists, Christians, Muslims, Jews, Mormons, and so on. My experience of engaging with this diverse group of students has been remarkable. In exploring the problem of evil and suffering, I try to make sure that my syllabus reflects the diversity of the class. We not only study the problem in world religions but also cover the topic from nonreligious perspectives. Despite the diverse views, engaging with the topic in a constructive way has been transforming for my students. Given the complex nature of the matter, many of my students often state that studying the subject from many different angles has made them more thoughtful toward other views, whether religious or atheist.

[8] For Hamza Yusuf Hanson's conversion story, see Zareena Grewal, *Islam Is a Foreign Country: American Muslims and the Global Crisis of Authority* (New York: New York University Press, 2014), 159–69.

[9] Annabel Nugent, "Yusuf/Cat Stevens Reveals the Near-Death Experience That Led Him to Convert to Islam," *Independent*, September 28, 2020, www.independent.co.uk/arts-entertainment/music/news/yusuf-cat-stevens-reveals-the-neardeath-experience-that-led-him-to-convert-to-islam-b672142.html.

INTRODUCTION

In my teachings and research, one thing that became apparent is that the Islamic view of evil and suffering is often missing from the academic literature on the topic. One can hardly find the writings of Muslim theologians as part of the anthologies on the subject. This monograph examines both theoretical and practical theodicy in Islamic theology along with case studies from the lives of Muslims. Particular attention is given to the American context. It aims to be a humble contribution to the field.

This book by no means represents the entire theology of Islam on the problem of evil and suffering. In order to provide a holistic picture, I employ a wide range of sources in the Islamic tradition including the Qur'an, hadith literature, jurisprudence (*fiqh*), poetry, the works of Sufi scholars, theologians, and philosophers. While I have tried to capture diverse approaches to the matter, my engagement is primarily limited to the Sunni scholars. Examining the works of major Shiite theologians as well as the perspectives of the key black Muslim American scholars in the context of evil and suffering is beyond the scope of this study. However, research on their readings of the sacred texts of Islam will advance this study and provide further nuances.

The readers will recognize that in addition to the sources in Arabic, I utilize the literature available in the Turkish language. The Turkish-speaking world has been and remains a major cultural zone of Islam. Employing the resources in Turkish can be considered as a strength of this work, because they are often dismissed or simply less known to the English-speaking academic world. I particularly engage with the works of Bediuzzaman Said Nursi (1876–1960), a Kurdish Muslim theologian, who wrote most of his works in the Arabic and Ottoman-Turkish languages. Nursi himself went through immense pain in his life. He witnessed and endured the suffering caused by World War I and II. Nursi was captured and held by Soviet Russia as a prisoner of war during World War I for two years. He lived in a time when the major tenets of faith were challenged because of the rise of communism as well as secularism.

INTRODUCTION

Nursi was exiled and imprisoned for more than thirty years because of his writings in modern Turkey. It was during those trying times that he composed his Qur'an commentary, *The Risale-i Nur* (The Book of Light). Because of his own context and experience, Nursi wrote extensively on the problem of evil and suffering in relation to God and human nature. When it is applicable, I refer to his works, which is another contribution of this study to the field. Also, for the discussions related to the articles of faith in Islam, I rely heavily on the relevant sections of my previous book, *Exploring Islam: Theology and Spiritual Practice in America*.[10]

I explore the matter in three parts. Part I introduces theoretical theodicy in four chapters. Chapter 1 outlines the problem of evil and suffering. What are evil and suffering? How do religious traditions such as Zoroastrianism, Hinduism, Buddhism, Judaism, and Christianity address the problem? What are the questions posed to traditional theism regarding evil and suffering? Chapter 2 discusses the notion of God in Islamic theology. It also looks at other supernatural beings such as angels, jinn, and Satan in the tradition. Some of the questions that I address in the chapter are the following: Who is God? What are the attributes of God? Who are angels and jinn? Who are humans in relation to God and angels?

Chapter 3 analyzes major theodicies for natural evil in Islamic theology. I review the positions of various theological schools such as the Mutazilites, Asharites, and Maturidis. The chapter also includes the views of Muslim scholars such as Ibn Sina, al-Arabi, al-Ghazali, Rumi, and Nursi. Chapter 4 concentrates on moral evil. I specifically evaluate the views of theological schools on the role of human agency in moral evil. Particular attention is given to the concepts of free will, acquisition (*kasb*), and predestination (*qadar* and *qada*).

In Part II, we try to understand the Muslim perspectives of practical theodicy. Chapter 5 explores aging in Islamic theology. What are

---

[10] Salih Sayilgan, *Exploring Islam: Theology and Spiritual Practice in America* (Minneapolis, MN: Fortress Press, 2021), 73–115.

8

the major questions about aging? How do sacred sources of Islam address these questions? What are the theological and spiritual responses to aging, loneliness, and filial piety? Chapter 6 focuses on the reception of sickness in Islam. Is sickness part of the creation of God? How are sickness and healing treated in the tradition? Chapter 7 reviews death, resurrection, and the hereafter in Islamic theology. How is death regarded in the sacred sources of Islam? Is there life after death? What are the major rituals of funerals and burial and how are they related to the problem of evil and suffering?

Part III addresses some of the contemporary cases. Chapter 8 explores how Islamic theology deals with disability. I look at the Qur'an and hadith literature on people with disabilities. How do Muslim scholars explain disability in relation to God's justice? I specifically shed light on blindness. Chapter 9 examines the environmental crisis and attempts to develop an Islamic ecological theology. I also highlight some environmental virtue ethics in Islam. Chapter 10 tries to understand the coronavirus (COVID-19) according to plagues and pandemics in Islamic literature.

Part I | God and the Problem of Evil

1 | Mapping the Problem

Simon Blackburn, a prominent British atheist philosopher, offers a compelling analogy to stress the problem of evil and suffering:

> Suppose you found yourself at school or university in a dormitory. Things are not too good. The roof leaks, there are rats about, the food is almost inedible, some students in fact starve to death. There is a closed door; behind which is the management, but the management never comes out. You get to speculate what the management must be like. Can you infer from the dormitory as you find it that the management, first, knows exactly what the conditions are like, second, cares intensely for your welfare, and third, possess unlimited resources for fixing things? The inference is crazy. You would be almost certain to infer that either the management doesn't know, doesn't care, or cannot do anything about it.[1]

With his comparison, Blackburn aims to demonstrate the inconsistency in the belief in a theistic God. God is often described as omnipotent, omniscient, and omnibenevolent in Judaism, Christianity, and Islam. Considering the evil and suffering that exist in the world, for Blackburn, this description is absurd. It is illogical because an all-powerful, all-knowing, and all-compassionate God would do something to eliminate evil and suffering in the world. As one would expect the management of the university to change the situation in the dormitory, so God should intervene to stop

---

[1] Simon Blackburn, *Think: A Compelling Introduction to Philosophy* (Oxford: Oxford University Press, 1999), 170.

13

PART I GOD AND THE PROBLEM OF EVIL

the suffering of people. Considering this challenge, this chapter explores the problem of evil and suffering. What are the concepts of evil and suffering? How do major religious traditions address the problem? What are the questions posed to traditional theism regarding evil and suffering? I begin with the definition of evil and suffering.

Theologians and philosophers have no consensus on definitions of evil and suffering. Evil is often described as something that is harmful, hurtful, undesirable, immoral, unjust, and sinful. Suffering is the outcome of evil. It is manifested in forms of sorrow, distress, physical pain, and mental illness.

Scholars have classified evil into different groups. The most common typologies are moral and natural evil. Moral evil is attributed to human beings as a result of the misuse of their free will. Some examples of moral evil are rape, child abuse, theft, genocide, murder, injustice, hatred, gossip, and dishonesty. In the case of natural evil, human agency is not involved. It is beyond human control and does not happen because of them – for example, earthquakes, floods, cancer, animal suffering, hurricanes, and birth defects.

There are also instances when moral and natural evil overlap. One example could be global warming. While it has a natural aspect, human agency is also involved. Floods can be seen as a form of natural evil; however, if people do not take the necessary measures, such events could become more destructive.

Religious Traditions on Evil and Suffering

The problem of evil and suffering is as old as human history. Why is there so much evil and suffering? Let alone bad people, why have good people, innocents, and animals faced suffering because of evil? Religions seek answers to these questions and provide explanations to their followers.

One of them is the ancient tradition of Zoroastrianism. It explains the problem of evil through its doctrine of dualism. According to this approach, there exist good and evil forces in the world, and they are at war with each other. The followers of Zoroastrianism believe that there is a wise lord (Ahura Mazda), whose army consists of angels and archangels, and an evil lord (Angra Mainyu), who is followed by demons and archdevils. All types of evil, including death, originate from the evil lord. The wise lord aims to eradicate evil and suffering in the world. The forces of good will eventually overcome evil and bring peace and prosperity to the world. While people have the freedom to choose between good and evil, they are taught to opt for good because their choices will determine the state of their lives in the hereafter. The consequence for them will be either heaven or hell.[2]

A similar approach to the problem of evil was articulated in Manichaeism, a tradition that dates to the third century CE. Like Zoroastrianism, Manichaeism also taught dualism. According to this doctrine, there are two natures in the universe: light and darkness. While light represents good and peace, darkness represents evil and conflict. The universe is the realm of struggle between good and evil forces, and there is not an omnipotent good power that dominates both. While God is the actor in the good realm, Satan represents the dominion of evil. Because it is part of the material world, humanity belongs to the realm of darkness; however, it has the capacity to be enlightened through the power of God. Therefore, humans are the battleground for both forces. Manichaeism's approach to evil and suffering appealed to many and spread from the Roman Empire to China.[3]

---

[2] For the teachings of Zoroastrianism, including its approach to the problem of evil, see S. A. Nigosian, *The Zoroastrian Faith: Tradition and Modern Research* (Montreal: McGill-Queen's University Press, 1993), 71–97.

[3] J. Kevin Coyle, *Manichaeism and Its Legacy* (Leiden: Brill, 2009), xiv–v. Also see "Manichaeism," in *The Columbia Encyclopedia*, by Paul Lagasse and Columbia University, 8th ed. (New York: Columbia University Press, 2018).

PART I GOD AND THE PROBLEM OF EVIL

Evil and Suffering in Major Dharmic Religions

The problem of evil and suffering has also remained a key question in Hinduism, the oldest dharmic tradition. One of the most important concepts related to evil and suffering in Hinduism is karma, the doctrine of cause and effect. According to this teaching, people suffer because of their actions. Good actions bring goodness, while bad actions cause suffering. Evil and suffering cannot be explained with reference to chance or accident. People are responsible for them. Their actions determine their present as well as future conditions.[4] Perhaps the most interesting aspect of this view is the lack of a divine power in the picture. That is why some major Western intellectuals, such as Max Weber and Peter Burger, found the doctrine of karma appealing. Weber, for example, wrote that "the most complete formal solution of the problem of theodicy is the special achievement of the Indian doctrine of *karma*, the so-called belief in the transmigration of souls. The world is viewed as a completely connected and self-contained cosmos of ethical retribution."[5] God is not involved in people's affairs concerning evil, as they create their own destinies. People's "fate in the successive lives of the soul" through multiple incarnations depends on their good and bad actions.[6] In this regard, for Weber, karma provides a reasonable answer for the sufferings of those who are innocent. Relying on Weber's approach to theodicy, Peter Berger also viewed the doctrine of karma as "the most rational" explanation among all theodicies. He noted that as part of the teaching of karma, "the individual has no one to blame for his misfortunes except himself – and conversely, he may ascribe his good fortune to nothing but his own merits."[7] According to this

---

[4] Huston Smith, *The World's Religions* (New York: HarperOne, 1991), 64–65.

[5] Max Weber, *The Sociology of Religion*, trans. Ephraim Fischoff (Boston: Beacon, 1993), 145.

[6] Weber, 145.

[7] Peter L. Berger, *The Sacred Canopy: Elements of a Sociological Theory of Religion* (New York: Anchor Books, 1969), 77.

MAPPING THE PROBLEM

interpretation, the power is in human hands. People have the sole agency over their actions as well as their destiny.

Perhaps no religion is concerned with the problem of evil and suffering as much as Buddhism. In fact, the story of Buddhism begins with this problem. Siddhartha Gautama – who came to be known as the Buddha after finding a profound answer to the question – was a prince enjoying an extravagant life in his father's palace. He was married and had a son. Getting bored with his luxurious life, the Buddha ventured out in a chariot accompanied by his charioteer a number of times. On his journey, the Buddha encountered four sights. The first three were an old man, a sick person in pain, and a dead body. When the Buddha asked his charioteer about them, he answered that these persons were going through the stages of life, and every human will go through the same phases. These three scenes of sickness, aging, and death dismantled the Buddha's joyful life. He realized that life is suffering as long as people go through these stages. In the fourth sighting, the Buddha saw an ascetic who did not have any material possessions and still looked happy and content in the midst of suffering. The ascetic inspired the Buddha and gave him hope to find an answer to suffering. He returned from the trip with a new understanding of reality. One night the Buddha left everything behind and embarked on a spiritual path of exploring a life without suffering. After the long journey of an ascetic life, and working with various teachers, the Buddha was enlightened and reached nirvana, the ideal spiritual state.

The Buddha then offered some guidelines for those who wanted to overcome suffering in life. However, he was uninterested in speculation. This is best reflected in one of the Buddhist parables. A monk was troubled by the Buddha's silence concerning the major questions of life, the nature of the world and body, and whether there is life after death. To prove how it is unnecessary to engage with metaphysical speculations, the Buddha gave an example of a man who was severely wounded by a poisoned arrow. People around him, including friends and

PART I GOD AND THE PROBLEM OF EVIL

relatives, wanted to take the man to a physician for immediate treatment. The Buddha then asked the monk to imagine that the man did not want the arrow removed until he knew who shot it, that person's clan, his appearance, his village, and why he shot it. What would happen? If he were to wait until all these questions were answered, the man would die. What matters in this situation is to get rid of the arrow to remove the pain and suffering.[8] That is why instead of being exhausted with speculation, the Buddha offered practical steps, the four noble truths, to deal with evil and suffering. The first step begins with the acknowledgment that there is suffering. This suffering is related not only to illness, old age, and death but also to emotional pain as well as suffering because of the impermanence of things. Being united with loved ones, for example, brings happiness; however, there is eventually separation. Impermanence is the nature of everything in this world, which leads to pain and suffering. The second noble truth is that suffering is caused by desires and attachments that are unsatisfied as well as ignorance – not knowing the nature of the things in the world. The third is that suffering can be transformed through detachment or by dismantling the disappointing desires. The fourth noble truth is that there is a path to liberating oneself from suffering. For this stage, the Buddha teaches specific ways to attain nirvana: (1) right view or understanding, (2) right resolve, (3) right speech, (4) right action, (5) right livelihood, (6) right effort, (7) right mindfulness, and (8) right concentration.[9] They are usually categorized as moral virtues, meditation, and wisdom. What is distinctive about Buddhism and Hinduism is that neither tradition makes any connection between a divine being and the problem of evil and suffering.

[8] Philip Novak, *The World's Wisdom: Sacred Texts of the World's Religions* (New York: HarperOne, 1994), 64.

[9] Christa W. Anbeek, "Evil and the Transformation of Evil in Buddhism and Socially Engaged Buddhism," in *Probing the Depths of Evil and Good: Multireligious Views and Case Studies*, ed. Jerald D. Gort et al. (Amsterdam: Rodopi, 2007), 104–5.

Evil and Suffering in Judaism and Christianity

Unlike the dharmic traditions, the Abrahamic religions engaged with the problem of evil and suffering in relation to a supreme being, God. God is the creator, he is the cause of all causes, he is omnibenevolent, omnipotent, and omniscient. There is nothing beyond his knowledge. Concerning God's attributes, the great Jewish philosopher and theologian Maimonides (d. 1204) wrote: "The foundation of all foundations and the pillar of wisdom is to know that there is a Primary Being who brought into being all existence. All the beings of the heavens, the earth, and what is between them came into existence only from the truth of His being." God is the creator of the world and the Lord of the entire earth: "He controls the sphere with infinite and unbounded power."[10]

God is also the source of morality. There is no duality in the universe either. This approach created questions about God concerning evil and suffering in the universe. Many Jewish theologians attempted to reconcile evil and suffering with God's justice. Maimonides, for example, pointed out that good dominates the world and evil is minor compared to it. God's "true kindness, and beneficence, and goodness" is evident in the world.[11] In addition, Maimonides classified evil into three categories: evil that is caused by nature, evil that people bring upon others, and self-inflicted evil.[12] For him, natural evil is necessary for the world and an essential part of God's plan. Maimonides also contested that asking why there is evil and suffering in the world is not the right question, because being part of the material world requires evil and suffering. A better question

---

[10] Moses Maimonides, "Yesodei haTorah: Chapter One," trans. Eliyahu Touger, Chabad.org, accessed January 12, 2022, www.chabad.org/library/article_cdo/aid/904960/jewish/Yesodei-haTorah-Chapter-One.htm.

[11] Moses Maimonides, *Guide for the Perplexed*, trans. M. Friedländer (London: Routledge, 1904), 268.

[12] Maimonides, 268–70.

PART I GOD AND THE PROBLEM OF EVIL

would be: "Why did God create us as part of this material world?" However, afflictions because of nature are still few in number:

> You will, nevertheless, find that the evils of the above kind which befall man are very few and rare: for you find countries that have not been flooded or burned for thousands of years: there are thousands of men in perfect health, deformed individuals are a strange and exceptional occurrence, or say few in number if you object to the term exceptional, – they are not one-hundredth, not even one-thousandth part of those that are perfectly normal.[13]

Maimonides also indicated that the second type of evil is not very common either: "It is of rare occurrence that a man plans to kill his neighbor or to rob him of his property by night. Many persons are, however, afflicted with this kind of evil in great wars: but these are not frequent, if the whole inhabited part of the earth is taken into consideration."[14]

He believed that self-inflicted evil is the root cause of most suffering in the world. This type of evil originates from people's excessive desires for things such as food, drink, and love. People indulge in these things disproportionately, which leads to "diseases and afflictions upon body and soul alike."[15] Humans are the victims of their own desires. In this regard, the origin of evil is people themselves. This approach is echoed in the words of Carl Gustav Jung (d. 1961): "We need more understanding of human nature, because the only real danger that exists is man himself. He is the great danger, and we are pitifully unaware of it. We know nothing of man, far too little. His psyche should be studied, because we are the origin of all coming evil."[16]

Saadia Gaon (d. 942), another Jewish philosopher, pointed out that God loves those who suffer. Making reference to the rabbinic

---

[13] Maimonides, 269.

[14] Maimonides, 269.

[15] Maimonides, 270.

[16] Murray Stein, ed., *Encountering Jung: Jung on Evil* (Princeton, NJ: Princeton University Press, 1996), 1.

MAPPING THE PROBLEM

doctrine of the sufferings of love, he maintained that God inflicts those whom he loves with unmerited sufferings in order to justify their eternal reward in the hereafter.[17] Saadia observed that there are three benefits of suffering. First, suffering is a means of character building. It is a way for people to be trained and disciplined. For this aspect of suffering, Saadia gives the example of a hardworking scholar: "We know from our own experience that one who is wise does burden himself with late hours and hard work, reading books, taxing his mental powers and discernment, to understand."[18] Such a scholar would experience difficulties on the journey because of that hard work. However, no one can argue that injustice is involved. Likewise, God brings suffering upon his people to form a better character in them.[19]

Second, suffering may be a punishment for the sin and wrongdoing of people. This type of suffering will purify people and bring them closer to their Creator:

> If a servant does commit an offense deserving punishment, part of the goodness of the All-Merciful and His watchfulness over His servants is in His causing some form of suffering to clear the transgressor's guilt wholly or in part. In such a case that suffering is called purgative: although it is a punishment, its object is that of grace, for it deters the transgressor from repeating his offenses and purifies him of those already committed.

To elaborate his point, Saadia provides the example of a father who would make his child "swallow bitter draughts and loathsome medicine to free him from illness or set right a distempered constitution." A skilled physician would do a similar thing to his patients.

---

[17] Lenn E. Goodman, "Judaism and the Problem of Evil," in *Cambridge Companion to the Problem of Evil*, ed. Chad Meister and Paul K. Moser (Cambridge: Cambridge University Press, 2017), 198.

[18] Saadiah ben Joseph al-Fayyumi, *The Book of Theodicy*, trans. Lenn E. Goodman (New Haven, CT: Yale University Press, 1988), 125.

[19] Saadiah, 125.

PART I GOD AND THE PROBLEM OF EVIL

In the process, the pain would be justified because it serves to "eliminate disease and harm."[20] Likewise, God inflicts his people with suffering so that they can advance spiritually.

Third, suffering is a form of test and trial for the innocent. If people turn to God in the midst of their suffering and remain patient, then they will receive a great reward in the hereafter: "An upright servant, whose Lord knows that he will bear sufferings loosed upon him and hold steadfast in his uprightness, is subjected to certain sufferings, so that when he steadfastly bears them, his Lord may reward and bless him. This too is a kind of bounty and beneficence, for it brings the servant to everlasting blessedness." For Saadia, the suffering of innocents falls within this category. This form of suffering is not unjust but rather an act of generosity and compassion. Saadia supports his point with the example of Job in the Hebrew Bible. He was tested and remained patient and faithful. As compensation, Job was "assured eternal bliss in the hereafter and granted far more than he had hoped for in this life."[21]

The problem of evil and suffering is a major theme of Christian theology as well. Like Judaism, the Christian tradition teaches God to be omnipotent, omniscient, and omnibenevolent. However, it also offers two distinct theological additions: a triune God and the doctrine of the original sin. In this regard, one of the most important concepts is atonement. While in the Hebrew Bible the concept is related to salvation, in Christian theology, it implies that there should be reconciliation between God and humans because of the original sin.[22] This sin originates from Adam and Eve. According to Saint Augustine (d. 430), while living in a perfect world as beings with freedom of choice, Adam and Eve disobeyed God and ate a forbidden fruit in the Garden of Eden. This event is known as the Fall in Christian theology. As a result of Adam and Eve's

[20] Saadiah, 125.
[21] Saadiah, 126.
[22] Paul S. Fiddes, "Christianity, Atonement and Evil," in Meister and Moser, *Cambridge Companion*, 215.

MAPPING THE PROBLEM

disobedience, every human being is born sinful, as they inherit a sinful state. Both moral and natural evil exist in the world because of the original sin.[23] The sin also created an estrangement between humans and God. To reconcile this, God became human through Jesus Christ to redeem people's sins and forgive them. In addition, the suffering of Jesus on the cross shows that God is not indifferent to people's suffering. God's justice will eventually be revealed in the hereafter. While those who were obedient will be saved through Christ and enjoy the eternal kingdom of God, the disobedient will be condemned to eternal punishment.[24] Augustine also pointed out that evil is the lack (privation) of goodness. It is not an entity and does not exist. He gives the example of diseases and wounds in animals. Their existence in the body of animals is the absence of health. Once they are recovered, diseases and wounds cease to exist instead of moving somewhere else.[25] Another example that Augustine provides is blindness, which is the absence of sight. It is not a thing in itself. Similarly, evil is not an entity and does not exist. It is a moving away from what is created as good through the freedom of the will.[26]

Another major theodicy came from Irenaeus, a Christian theologian who lived in the second century CE. Unlike Augustine, Irenaeus believed that while this world is the best possible world, it is still imperfect because humans have not fully developed yet. Their development and progress toward perfection require free will and the existence of evil and suffering.[27] The English theologian and philosopher John Hick (d. 2012) later expanded on the theodicy of

---

[23] Fiddes, 213.

[24] Chad V. Meister, *Evil: A Guide for the Perplexed* (New York: Bloomsbury, 2012), 30–31.

[25] Vernon Joseph Bourke, *The Essential Augustine* (Indianapolis: Hackett, 1974), 65–66.

[26] Chad V. Meister, "The Problem of Evil," in *Cambridge Companion to Christian Philosophical Theology*, ed. Charles Taliaferro and Chad V. Meister (Cambridge: Cambridge University Press, 2009), 160.

[27] John Hick, *Evil and the God of Love* (New York: Palgrave Macmillan, 2010), 211–15.

PART I GOD AND THE PROBLEM OF EVIL

Irenaeus in his *Evil and the God of Love*. He pointed out that God permits evil and suffering in the world to form humans into moral beings, which will enable them to follow God's will. God did not create humans as perfect, because the perfection that is achieved through trials and tribulations is more valuable than initial perfection. Hick uses the analogy of a parent and their child. While a loving parent would like to see their child be happy, in some cases they may also like to see their child struggle because it is through challenges that the child will be able to embody values such as "moral integrity, unselfishness, compassion, courage, humour, reverence for the truth, and perhaps above all the capacity for love."[28] Hick's approach is known as the soul-making theodicy.

Challenges to the Theistic View of Evil and Suffering

Evil and suffering have remained not only a religious problem but also a nonreligious one. Many philosophers have pointed out that the idea of a powerful, just, and loving God cannot be reconciled with the evil and suffering that exist in the world. For many atheists, there is a logical inconsistency in believing in a theistic God because of evil and suffering.

The Logical Problem of Evil

Epicurus (d. 270 BCE), an ancient Greek philosopher, was one of the earliest advocates of the logical problem of evil. For him, the idea of a powerful, merciful, and perfectly good God who knows everything is logically inconsistent with the evil and suffering that exist in the world: "Either God wants to abolish evil, and cannot; or he can, but does not want to. If he wants to, but cannot, he is impotent. If he can, but does not want to, he is wicked. If God can abolish evil, and God

---

[28] Hick, 258.

MAPPING THE PROBLEM

really wants to do it, why is there evil in the world?"[29] David Hume (d. 1776), one of the most influential philosophers of the Enlightenment, articulated similar reasoning: "Is God willing to prevent evil, but not able? Then he is impotent. Is he able, but not willing? Then he is malevolent. Is he both able and willing? Whence then is evil?"[30]

John Stuart Mill (d. 1873) also raised questions concerning the problem of evil and suffering. Mill did not see the manifestation of a merciful God in the world; he saw a cruel one: "Not even on the most distorted and contracted theory of good whichever was framed by religious or philosophical fanaticism can the government of nature be made to resemble the work of a being at once good and omnipotent."[31] To Mill, there is also no justice in the world:

> If the law of all creation were justice and the creator omnipotent then, in whatever amount suffering and happiness might be dispensed to the world, each person's share of them would be exactly proportioned to that person's good or evil deeds; no human being would have a worse lot than another, without worse deserts; accident or favoritism would have no part in such a world, but every human life would be the playing out of a drama constructed like a perfect moral tale.[32]

However, Mill concludes:

> No one is able to blind himself to the fact that the world we live in is totally different from this; in so much that the necessity of redressing the balance has been deemed one of the strongest arguments for another life after death, which amounts to an admission that the order of things in this life is often an example of injustice, not justice.[33]

---

[29] Quoted in Meister, *Evil*, 6.

[30] David Hume, *Dialogues Concerning Natural Religion*, ed. Martin Bell (London: Penguin, 1991), 108–9.

[31] John Stuart Mill, *Three Essays on Religion: Nature, the Utility of Religion, and Theism* (London: Longmans, Green, Reader, and Dyer, 1874), 38.

[32] Mill, 37–38.

[33] Mill, 38.

PART I GOD AND THE PROBLEM OF EVIL

The fact that many people believe in the idea of compensation in the hereafter because of their sufferings indicates that there is no justice and compassion in this world. Charles Darwin (d. 1882) was not indifferent to the evil and suffering in the creation either. He was especially troubled by animal suffering: "Some have attempted to explain this in reference to man by imagining that it serves for his moral improvement. But the number of men in the world is as nothing compared with that of all other sentient beings, and these often suffer greatly without any moral improvement." Darwin then questions: "For what advantage can there be in the sufferings of millions of the lower animals throughout almost endless time?"[34] To Darwin, the suffering of animals and the idea of a benevolent God are incompatible.

The logical problem of evil became widely known with the work of Australian philosopher J. L. Mackie (d. 1981). Mackie maintains that the problem of evil provides sufficient evidence against the existence of a theistic God. His argument can be summarized as follows:

- God is omnipotent.
- God is omniscient.
- God is omnibenevolent.
- Evil exists.

Mackie maintains that some of these premises could be true, but it is impossible to say that all of them are accurate at the same time because they are logically inconsistent. If God is omnipotent, he is able to prevent evil and suffering that exist in the world; if God is omniscient, he knows how to eliminate the evil and suffering; if God is omnibenevolent, then he is also willing to remove evil and suffering from the world. A compassionate God would care about the sufferings of people. Despite all these attributes, evil and

[34] Nora Barlow, ed., *The Autobiography of Charles Darwin, 1809–1882* (New York: W. W. Norton, 1993), 90.

suffering exist. The conclusion is that a god with these attributes does not exist. Mackie also disagrees with the idea of free will as an explanation for the problem of evil. God could create beings who could always choose good. If this is a possibility, why did God not create individuals who would not choose to do evil? The freedom that these creatures enjoy should not have come at the price of the evil and suffering that exist in the world.[35]

One of the most profound responses to Mackie's challenge came from Alvin Plantinga, an American philosopher and theologian who was awarded the Templeton Prize in 2017 for his work in defense of religion in general and Christianity in particular. Plantinga describes his objection as the "free will defense." In his *God, Freedom, and Evil*, Plantinga maintains that the idea of a theistic God and the fact that evil exists in the world are compatible given the concept of free will. First, a world in which there are beings "who are significantly free (and freely perform more good than evil actions) is more valuable, all else being equal, than a world containing no free creatures at all."[36] Second, if God is the creator of free beings, one cannot expect him to intervene in their freedom. In this case, these mortals would not enjoy significant freedom. In other words, creating free beings who are committed to moral good would come at the expense of their capability to do evil. Some of God's creatures choose evil because of their freedom, which is the source of moral evil. However, one cannot argue that this is incompatible with God's omnipotence and omnibenevolence because God could merely prevent moral evil "only by removing the possibility of moral good."[37]

Plantinga attempts to explain natural evil with the same reasoning. Expanding on Augustine's traditional doctrine of the original

---

[35] J. L. Mackie, "Evil and Omnipotence," *Mind* 64:254 (1955): 200–12.

[36] Alvin C. Plantinga, *God, Freedom, and Evil* (Grand Rapids, MI: William B. Eerdmans, 1977), 30.

[37] Plantinga, 30.

PART I GOD AND THE PROBLEM OF EVIL

sin, Plantinga argues that natural evil can possibly be attributed to free nonhuman spirits such as Satan and his cohorts:

> Satan, so the traditional doctrine goes, is a mighty nonhuman spirit who, along with many other angels, was created long before God created man. Unlike most of his colleagues, Satan rebelled against God and since has been wreaking whatever havoc he can. The result of this is natural evil. So the natural evil we find is due to free actions of nonhuman spirits.[38]

Plantinga then points out that it is possible to argue that:

> [N]atural evil is due to the free actions of nonhuman persons; there is a balance of good over evil with respect to the actions of these nonhuman persons; and it was not within the power of God to create a world that contains a more favorable balance of good over evil with respect to the actions of nonhuman persons it contains.[39]

It is often believed that Plantinga provided the most challenging response to the logical problem of evil.

The Evidential Problem of Evil

Many atheists not only find the theistic view of God and the existence of evil incompatible; they also point to the evidential problem of evil and suffering. One of the key arguments of theism has been that evil and suffering often lead to a greater good. However, according to atheistic views, it is impossible to justify evil and suffering since so much of it is unnecessary. Disproportionate evil often leads to more destruction, not the greater good. One of the proponents of this argument is William L. Rowe (d. 2015). To support his position, Rowe provides two compelling cases of animal

---

[38] Plantinga, 58.
[39] Plantinga, 58.

MAPPING THE PROBLEM

and human suffering. For animal suffering, Rowe gives the example of a baby deer trapped in a forest fire caused by lightning. It is "horribly burned, and lies in terrible agony for several days before death relieves its suffering."[40] The other example is even more horrifying. It is the story of a five-year-old girl in Flint, Michigan, who was raped and brutally killed on New Year's Day in 1986.[41]

According to Rowe, if there were a being who is all-powerful and all-good at the same time, he would not permit the suffering of this innocent child and the deer. If this being could not prevent their suffering for the sake of a greater good, that means this being is not all-powerful, all-knowing, and all-good. That also means such a being does not exist.[42] Expanding on Rowe's evidential problem of evil, Paul Draper concludes that the God presented by the theists does not exist. Draper points out that a better approach would be to think that if there is a God, it appears that he is indifferent to the suffering of creatures. This is more plausible than the theistic view of God because there is disproportionate evil and suffering in the world that cannot be explained by the idea of a greater good.[43]

One of the most vivid pictures of unjustified evil is presented by Fyodor Dostoyevsky (d. 1881) in his *The Brothers Karamazov* through the arguments of its major character, Ivan. Dostoyevsky addresses the suffering of innocent children. In one example, Ivan illustrates two examples. One of them is the story of a five-year-old girl who is severely tortured by her parents:

> They beat her, thrashed her, kicked her for no reason till her body was one bruise. Then, they went to greater refinements of cruelty – shut

---

[40] William L. Rowe, "The Problem of Evil and Some Varieties of Atheism," *American Philosophical Quarterly* 16:4 (1979): 337.

[41] William L. Rowe, "Evil and Theodicy," *Philosophical Topics* 16:2 (1988): 119.

[42] Rowe, 120–26.

[43] For Paul Draper's view on the evidential problem of evil, see Paul Draper, "God, Evil, and the Nature of Light," in Meister and Moser, *Cambridge Companion*, 65–84; and Paul Draper, "Pain and Pleasure: An Evidential Problem for Theists," *Nous* 23:3 (1989): 331–50.

PART I GOD AND THE PROBLEM OF EVIL

her up all night in the cold and frost in a privy, and because she didn't ask to be taken up at night (as though a child of five sleeping its angelic, sound sleep could be trained to wake and ask), they smeared her face and filled her mouth with excrement, and it was her mother, her mother did this. And that mother could sleep, hearing the poor child's groans![44]

The other story is of a general who tortured an eight-year-old boy. The general loved dogs. One day while playing, a serf boy threw a rock that hurt the paw of the general's favorite hound. Learning that his hound had become lame because of the boy, he ordered the child to be taken from his mother and locked up all night. Dostoyevsky describes this tragic event as follows: "Early that morning the general comes out on horseback, with the hounds, his dependents, dog-boys, and huntsmen, all mounted around him in full hunting parade. The servants are summoned for their edification, and in front of them all stands the mother of the child." The general then orders the child to be brought up and undressed: "The child is stripped naked. He shivers, numb with terror, not daring to cry. ... 'Make him run,' commands the general. 'Run! run!' shout the dog-boys. The boy runs. ... 'At him!' yells the general, and he sets the whole pack of hounds on the child. The hounds catch him, and tear him to pieces before his mother's eyes!"[45]

Given the amount of evil and suffering in the world, Ivan opposes some of the traditional theodicies. First, he raises questions about the original sin and the suffering of children. How can their suffering be justified because of the original sin? Why should they suffer because of their fathers' sin? He points out that "the innocent must not suffer for another's sin, especially such innocents."[46] Second, Ivan complains that despite the innocent children's prayer to God to protect

---

[44] Fyodor Dostoyevsky, *The Brothers Karamazov*, trans. Constance Garnett (New York: Modern Library, n.d.), 287.

[45] Dostoyevsky, 288.

[46] Dostoyevsky, 282.

MAPPING THE PROBLEM

them, there is no explanation as to why God did not protect them. Third, it is often told that evil and good are the cost of being created on the earth. Ivan then asks why the creation should have an enormous cost. Fourth, Ivan challenges the idea of having justice and compensation in the hereafter. He cries for justice on the earth, "not in some remote infinite time and space."[47] The eternal harmony that religion promises comes with a great price, and it should not be built on the suffering of innocent children. Ivan remarks that he would hasten to return a ticket to an eternal peaceful place called the hereafter. Ivan then poses a question to his religious brother, Alyosha:

> Imagine that you are creating a fabric of human destiny with the object of making men happy in the end, giving them peace and rest at last, but that it was essential and inevitable to torture to death only one tiny creature—that baby beating its breast with its fist, for instance—and to found that edifice on its unavenged tears, would you consent to be the architect on those conditions? Tell me, and tell the truth.[48]

He implies that no one would like to be the creator of a world where innocents suffer for other people's happiness.

Evil and suffering is the major theme of Albert Camus's (d. 1960) *The Plague* as well. The novel relates the story of a deadly plague that breaks out in the French Algerian city of Oran. Many residents of the town die, and people live in isolation for months. It is a painful situation for them. The novel highlights the fragility of life, which is constantly subject to suffering, death, and destruction. But it also underlines that there is no meaning in evil and the suffering of the people. Their suffering is unnecessary. Camus articulates this view mainly through his major character Bernard Rieux, the medical doctor of the town working to treat people. In many ways, his role is similar to Dostoyevsky's Ivan. Dr. Rieux disputes the idea of a powerful God who can cure people. In response to the question of

---

[47] Dostoyevsky, 289.
[48] Dostoyevsky, 291.

PART I GOD AND THE PROBLEM OF EVIL

whether he believes in the Christian God, Rieux responds that if he believed in "an all-powerful God," he "would cease curing the sick and leave that to Him."[49] For Rieux, there is no meaning behind death. The best response is to fight it: "But, since the order of the world is shaped by death, mightn't it be better for God if we refuse to believe in Him and struggle with all our might against death, without raising our eyes toward the heaven where He sits in silence."[50] Even if God exists, he is silent and indifferent to the suffering of people. So why should we wait for an answer for our suffering from such God? Like Dostoyevsky's Ivan, Rieux brings up the suffering of innocents. He is disturbed and angered by the suffering of a child whom he tried to do everything to treat. It is difficult for Rieux to bear the last moments of the child's life. Fr. Paneloux, the priest of the town, is also present at the time. There is a dialogue between the two. Fr. Paneloux asks Dr. Rieux, "Why was there that anger in your voice just now? What we'd been seeing was as unbearable to me as it was to you." Rieux answers, "I know. I'm sorry. But weariness is a kind of madness. And there are times when the only feeling I have is one of mad revolt." Fr. Paneloux then responds, "I understand, that sort of thing is revolting because it passes our human understanding. But perhaps we should love what we cannot understand."[51] Dr. Rieux reacts, "No, Father. I've a very different idea of love. And until my dying day I shall refuse to love a scheme of things in which children are put to torture."[52] Dr. Rieux does not believe that he should blindly accept the suffering of innocent children, leave the matter to God, and think of it as a divine act. One can trace the influence of Friedrich Nietzsche (d. 1900) on Camus. In his *On the Genealogy of Morality*, Nietzsche points to the meaninglessness and absurdity of evil and suffering. He believes that looking at

---

[49] Albert Camus, *The Plague*, trans. Stuart Gilbert (New York: Modern Library, 1948), 116.

[50] Camus, 117–18.

[51] Camus, 196.

[52] Camus, 196–97.

the problem of evil from a theistic perspective prevents people from being creative and making progress to change their situation.[53]

One of the most interesting challenges to the problem of evil and suffering came from William R. Jones (d. 2012), an African American philosopher. Jones grew up in the Baptist Church. He later joined the Unitarian and Universalists and became an ordained minister. Jones specialized in liberation theology and religious humanism. He taught religion at Yale Divinity School and Florida State University for many years.

Known as a secular humanist, Jones devoted most of his work to the suffering of black people in America. However, he found the black theology of his time to be problematic. In line with the traditional Christian theology, black theologians supported the idea of a God who is good and on the side of the black people who suffer. These black theologians preached that "the harder the cross, the brighter the crown." Jones calls their approach "Whiteanity."[54] For them, this life is the realm of test and suffering, and black people should be patient in their suffering because God will eventually reward them with a "brighter crown" in the hereafter.[55]

Jones considers this approach as an obstacle to making the situation of black people better. If God was omnibenevolent and involved in human history, one cannot help but think of him as a white racist – or in the case of the Holocaust, an anti-Semite. This is because the suffering of some ethnic groups, especially black people, is enormously disproportionate. Jones also questions the viewpoint of a greater good in evil and suffering. In the case of black suffering, it is difficult to support this argument: "Suffering unto death, for instance, negates any interpretation of pedagogical suffering; i.e., we learn from a burn to avoid fire. This makes no sense if the learning method destroys

---

[53] Friedrich Nietzsche, *On the Genealogy of Morality*, trans. Carol Diethe (Cambridge: Cambridge University Press, 2007), 68–120 and 145–57.

[54] William R. Jones, *Is God a White Racist? A Preamble to Black Theology* (Boston: Beacon, 1997), vii.

[55] Jones, ix.

PART I GOD AND THE PROBLEM OF EVIL

the learner."[56] For Jones, there is no greater good in the suffering of black people because the suffering often destroys them.

Instead of a God who is omnibenevolent and involved in human history, Jones offers a humanocentric theism and secular humanism: "The essential feature of both is the advocacy of the functional ultimacy of man. Man must act as if he were the ultimate valuator or the ultimate agent in human history or both. Thus God's responsibility for the crimes and errors of human history is reduced if not effectively eliminated."[57] From this perspective, humans are the creators of their actions and history, and they have a responsibility to change their own situation. The humanocentric approach is also a proposal against quietism. Black people often accepted their suffering and remained silent in the hope of a better life in the hereafter:

> The oppressed, in part, are oppressed precisely because they buy, or are indoctrinated to accept, a set of beliefs that negate those attitudes and actions necessary for liberation. Accordingly, the purpose and first step of a theology of liberation is to effect a radical conversion of the mind of the oppressed, to free his/her mind from those destructive and enslaving beliefs that stifle the movement toward liberation.[58]

Jones maintains that his humanocentric method aims to motivate black people to be active and fight against the injustices they face.[59]

The question of evil and suffering has generated a remarkable collection of literature. Followers of religious traditions, atheism, and agnosticism have engaged with the issue creatively. However, the notion of God in relation to the world remains the main theme of their discussions. This is the subject of Chapter 2, from an Islamic theological perspective.

[56] Jones, 22.
[57] Jones, xxvii.
[58] Jones, 41.
[59] In his book *Islam and the Problem of Black Suffering* (Oxford University Press, 2014), Sherman A. Jackson draws on the work of Jones. Jackson puts Islamic perspectives of theodicy in conversation with Jones's idea of "humanocentric theism" and attempts to make space for a protest-oriented approach in Islamic theology of theodicy.

2 | God, Angels, Humans, and Satan

Salahuddin Jitmoud, an American Muslim, was stabbed to death and robbed in an apartment complex in Lexington, Kentucky, in April 2015. He was making pizza deliveries. What is notable about Salahuddin's case is how his father, Abdul Munim Sombat Jitmoud, treated the person who killed his son. Abdul Munim moved to the United States with his family from Thailand and served as the principal of a number of Islamic schools in various states, including Kentucky. During a court hearing in 2017, Abdul Munim turned to the man convicted of the murder of his son and stated that he forgave him:

> My son, my nephew, I forgive you. I forgive you on behalf of Salahuddin and his mother. I don't blame you for the crime you have committed. I am not angry at you for being a part of hurting my son. I am angry at the devil. I blame the devil, who misguided you and misled you to do such a horrible crime. Forgiveness is the greatest gift or charity in Islam.[1]

The father not only forgave the convict, he also stepped forward and hugged him. He noted that one of the verses of the Qur'an that he often turned to for comfort was: "Say, 'Nothing will happen to us

---

[1] Marva Eltagouri, "Why This Father Hugged the Man Who Helped Kill His Son," *Washington Post*, November 10, 2017, www.washingtonpost.com/news/acts-of-faith/wp/2017/11/10/why-this-father-hugged-the-man-who-helped-kill-his-son/. Also see Jitmoud's talk, "Why I Hugged My Son's Killer? Abdul Munim Sombat Jitmoud," Muslim Community Center – MCC East Bay, YouTube video, posted August 12, 2021, www.youtube.com/watch?v=uPT6X57fBL4.

PART I GOD AND THE PROBLEM OF EVIL

except what God has decreed for us. He is our Protector, and in God let the believers put their trust.'"[2] In addition, Abdul Munim pointed out that he advised the convict to turn to God, who is the most forgiving. The following verse from the Qur'an became an inspiration for Abdul Munim to forgive the killer of his son: "Let them pardon and forgive. Do you not wish that God should forgive you? God is Forgiving and Merciful."[3] Abdul Munim's faith in God led him to this remarkable forgiveness. Because of his outstanding example of compassion, Abdul Munim received Malaysia's first Compassion Award icon from the Ministry of Religious Affairs in 2019.[4] The award is known as "mercy to all people" (*rahmatan lil alamin*), a reference from the Qur'an indicating that God sent Muhammad as a mercy for all creatures.[5] So who is the God of Muslims? How do Muslims relate to their divinity? This chapter examines the concept of God and his attributes in Islamic theology. I also explore the roles of humans, angels, and Satan in relation to the Creator.

While Muslims refer to God by many different names, the most common name used to invoke or address and praise God is Allah. Arabic-speaking Jews and Christians also use this word, which derives from the combination of the Arabic article *al* and the word *ilah*. In this regard, Allah literally means "the God." Grammatically speaking, the word Allah has no plural form or associated gender.

Islamic tradition relates that in Mecca, the birthplace of Islam, people already had a notion of Allah but associated other gods with him. While the Meccans considered Allah to be their supreme creator, they also believed that other deities existed that interceded between them and Allah. Islamic tradition dates the history of Mecca to Abraham, his concubine Hagar, and his son Ishmael,

---

[2] Qur'an 9:51.

[3] Qur'an 24:22.

[4] Azura Abas, "Forgiving US Father Receives Malaysia's Compassionate Icon Award," *New Straits Times*, December 19, 2019, www.nst.com.my/news/nation/2019/12/549299/forgiving-us-father-receives-malaysias-compassionate-icon-award.

[5] Qur'an 21:107.

who brought monotheism to Mecca. But it is believed that at some point, through interactions with neighboring cities, Mecca was introduced to polytheism. By the dawn of Islam, the Kaaba – built by Abraham and his family as the house of the one God – was full of deities. With the coming of Islam, Arab society was reintroduced to its monotheistic roots and the belief in one God, or Allah. But who is this God whom Muslims worship?

To understand and know the ways of God, Muslims turn to three sources: the Qur'an, the Prophet Muhammad, and the created universe itself. When trying to comprehend God, Muslims believe that one should first look at the creation. The Qur'an relates the following verse: "I [God] created jinn and humankind only that they might worship me."[6] The purpose of creation is to know, worship, and remember God. This form of worship and remembrance is by choice, not force. Some of the Qur'an commentaries interpret the phrase "only to worship Me" as "only to know me." In line with this interpretation, a widely circulated sacred narration (*hadith al-qudsi*) reports that God said, "I was a hidden treasure, and I loved to be known; so I created creation in order to be known."[7] In the center of the story of the creation stands God's desire to reveal and introduce himself.

A few analogies might help us to understand the Islamic theology of creation. Perhaps one of the most enjoyable things for artists is to exhibit their work. Through their exhibits, artists not only delight in seeing their pieces displayed but also enjoy visitors' appreciation and admiration. For teachers, one of the most pleasing things is to show their knowledge and share it with an audience. In the same way, people who are beautiful or perfect in some way or possess specific knowledge and skills naturally aim to reveal, display, and manifest these qualities and abilities. They would especially like

---

[6] Qur'an 51:56.

[7] Joseph E. B. Lumbard, "Commentary on *Surat al-Dhariyat*," in Nasr et al., *Study Quran*, 1280. A *hadith al-qudsi* is a report that is attributed to God from the perspective of its meaning, but it is articulated with the words of the Prophet Muhammad.

PART I GOD AND THE PROBLEM OF EVIL

to express their skills to those capable of both understanding and offering a proper response.[8] From an Islamic point of view, knowledge, love, and worship of the creator make up that appropriate response. God exhibits his large treasure of skills and blessings in this universe and invites his creation, particularly humans, to freely and consciously acknowledge him as their only creator. That, in short, is the main purpose of creation in Islam.

God's Names: *Asma al-Husna*

The most important way of knowing God is through his most beautiful names (*asma al-husna*). God reveals himself through these names, which the Qur'an refers to as follows: "The most beautiful names belong to God, so call on Him by them."[9] In another verse, the Qur'an instructs its followers to "call upon God, or the Compassionate – whatever names you call Him, the most beautiful names belong to Him."[10] The Qur'an repeatedly mentions God by different names and attributes. In chapter 59, for example, many of God's names are listed together:

> He is God, there is no god other than Him; who knows all things both secret and open. He is the Most Beneficent, the Most Merciful. He is God, there is no god other than Him, the Controller, the Holy One, the Source of Peace, the Guardian of Faith, the Preserver of Safety, the Exalted in Might, the Irresistible, the Supreme. Glory be to God, He is above all that they associate as partners with Him. He is God, the Creator, the Evolver, the Fashioner, to Him belong the most beautiful names. Everything in the heavens and earth glorifies Him. He is the Mighty, the Wise.[11]

---

[8] Said Nursi, *Sözler* (Istanbul: Söz Basim, 2009), 178.
[9] Qur'an 7:180.
[10] Qur'an 17:110.
[11] Qur'an 59:22–24.

38

GOD, ANGELS, HUMANS, AND SATAN

While Islamic literature often references the ninety-nine names of God, the Qur'an mentions more than a hundred. Therefore, the number ninety-nine should not be taken literally, since scripture contains more than that. All chapters of the Qur'an except one begin with the names of God, al-Rahman and al-Rahim, the most compassionate and the most merciful. God is al-Khaliq, the one who brings everything from nonexistence to existence. God is al-'Adl, the embodiment of justice. God is al-'Alim, the all-knowing one; there is nothing beyond his knowledge. God is al-Razzaq, the provider. God is al-Latif, the most gracious one. God is al-Ghafur, the all-forgiving one. God is al-Wadud, the all-loving one. God is al-Mumit, the one who inflicts death. God is also al-Muhyi, the one who gives life. God is al-Quddus, the most holy one – the one who is pure and without imperfection. The self-cleansing of the universe through alteration, transformation, death, and recreation is regarded as the manifestation of this name. God is also al-Qayyum, the self-sufficient one, who depends on nothing but on whom everything depends.

The Qur'an refers to this attribute of God with the following verse:

> God: there is no god but He, the Living, the Self-Subsisting. Neither slumber nor sleep overtakes Him. His are all things in the heavens and on the earth. Who is there that can intercede with Him except by His permission? He knows what is before them and what is behind them, but they do not comprehend of His knowledge except what He wills. His throne encompasses the heavens and the earth, and their preservation does not tire Him. He is the Exalted, the Magnificent.[12]

Muslims often know this verse by heart and usually recite it in their daily supplications.

---

[12] Qur'an 2:255.

PART I GOD AND THE PROBLEM OF EVIL

God's Essence, Attributes, and Acts

Muslim theologians have classified God's names in numerous ways. One way is to think of God's names as being related to his essence (*dhat*), attributes (*sifat*), and acts (*af'al*). The names concerning God's essence belong only to him – there is nothing created that can share the qualities enumerated by these names. In this regard, the Qur'an affirms, "There is nothing like Him."[13] Among the attributes of his essence is existence (*wujud*). Thus God's existence stems from himself. He is not created, and his existence depends on nothing. Everything will perish except God. God has neither beginning nor end.

Another way to categorize God's names is by his attributes (*sifat*), such as power (*qudra*), knowledge (*'ilm*), will (*irada*), life (*hayat*), speech (*kalam*), hearing (*sam'*), and sight (*basar*). While these attributes are unlimited in God, humans can only partially embody these names. For example, whereas God is all-knowing, humans have limited knowledge. Whereas God has life without imperfection, humans and other creatures have life only because of God. Their life depends on God and is subject to imperfections, including illness and death. God also has the attribute of will (*irada*). Human beings share this attribute, but while God's will is unlimited, humans' free will is highly limited.

Other names relate to God's active role (*af'al*) in the creation (*khalq*) of the universe. Everything is created by God. God creates the universe from nothing (*insha*). He gives life (*ihya*) as well as death (*imata*). As part of his active role, God is also the one who provides (al-Razzaq) for his creation. In order for his creatures to continue living, God meets all their needs.

God's Nearness and Distance

To understand God's essence and attributes, Muslim theologians point to his nearness and distance. The Qur'an states that everything

---

[13] Qur'an 42:11.

40

GOD, ANGELS, HUMANS, AND SATAN

is near to God and in his control: "To God belong the East and the West. Wherever you turn, there is the presence of God. No leaf falls without His knowledge."[14] In another verse, God's nearness to humankind is stated: "We are nearer to him than his jugular vein."[15] But Islamic theology also emphasizes God's distance from the creation. God is everywhere, so no particular thing or place is associated with God. In emphasizing God's distance, the Qur'an states that angels ascend to God "on a day whose measure is fifty thousand years."[16] One hadith reports that God is behind 7,000 veils.[17] God is close to creation through the manifestations of his names and attributes, while the creation itself is distant from God's essence.[18]

God's Jamali and Jalali Names

Islamic theology speaks of the two modes of God, or his dual nature. God's names are also divided into beauty and mercy (jamali) and glory and majesty (jalali) aspects. Jamali names are manifested in the universe as beauty, mercy, compassion, forgiveness, love, and kindness. The beauty of the creation – with its distinctive forms, fashions, and colors – generosity, and blessings are also among these names. Others are the Most Beautiful (al-Jamil), the Most Generous (al-Karim), and the Giver of Life (al-Muhyi).

The jalali names are revealed in the forms of majesty, awe, and fear. Life, light, and existence are manifestations of the jalali names, as are death, separation, fear, punishment, wrath, and major natural disasters. These names include the Majestic/Exalted (al-Jalil), the Subduer (al-Qahhar), the Almighty (al-Aziz), the Bringer of Death (al-Mumit), the Avenger (al-Muntaqim), and the Compeller (al-Jabbar).

---

[14] Qur'an 2:115; 6:59.
[15] Qur'an 50:16.
[16] Qur'an 70:4.
[17] Nursi, Sözler, 277.
[18] Said Nursi, The Words (Istanbul: Sözler, 2006), 215.

PART I GOD AND THE PROBLEM OF EVIL

In the universe, one can also observe that the *jamali* names are revealed within the *jalali* names. For example, within God's unity (*wahdaniyya*) is the manifestation of divine oneness (*ahadiyya*). As the light of the sun encompasses the entire earth, so does God's glory and unity. As the sun's light, heat, colors, and shadows are found in transparent objects and drops of water, so are God's *jalal* and oneness. God is present in the universe and is the provider for all of creation. But God is also particular in providing according to the distinctive needs of every being. All the flowers on earth together, for example, manifest God's glory and unity. However, every single flower, with its distinctive beauty and color, manifests God's *jamal* and oneness.

The *jalali* names will be fully revealed in hell, while the *jamali* names will have their full manifestation in heaven. However, God's mercy is emphasized over his wrath. In one of the *hadith al-qudsi*, God says, "My mercy overcomes my wrath."[19] The Qur'an also stresses God's mercy: "Your Lord has prescribed mercy upon Himself, if any of you did evil in ignorance, and thereafter repented, and amend his conduct, indeed He is Forgiving and Merciful."[20] Referring to the coming of the Prophet Muhammad, the Qur'an notes that he was sent as a mercy to all creatures.[21]

Humankind in Relation to God and His Names

At the center of the theology of God's names is humankind. Unlike in the Christian tradition, the notion of original sin is absent in Islamic theology. God created Adam and Eve, and they slipped "individually," as the Qur'an puts it. Both repented, and God eventually forgave them. The Qur'an points out that Adam and Eve were abiding in heaven. God gave them permission to do anything

---

[19] Muslim b. al-Hajjaj, *Sahih Muslim: kitab al-tawbah, bab fi sa'ah rahmah allah ta'ala.* The hadiths are cited according to the chapter, subchapter system.
[20] Qur'an 6:54.
[21] Qur'an 21:107.

42

GOD, ANGELS, HUMANS, AND SATAN

except approach a particular tree. Satan tempted them with the idea of becoming eternal if they ate fruit from the forbidden tree.[22]

Humans are the mirror of God's names in the most comprehensive way. That is why they are – along with the Qur'an and universe – also seen as a book to be read in relation to God. According to a hadith that often appears in Sufi literature, "God created humankind in his image."[23] Humankind was not only created in the image of God, but humans are the ones who read and contemplate God's names better than any being in the universe.

In the story of the creation in Islam, one learns that "Adam was taught the names" by which humans are made superior even to the angels. The ability to recognize the manifestation of God's names in creation is one of the most important ways to know God. To believe that there is one God is different from knowing God. Once humans know God and have knowledge of him, they will be led to have admiration as well as love for him. Love for God is followed by strong faith and worship. In this regard, contemplating the universe in relation to God (*tafakkur*) is an act of worship.

Being the Mirror of God's Names

Humans not only reflect on the names of God and have the ability to contemplate their manifestations in the universe; they also have the responsibility to embody God's names in their acts. In line with the Qur'anic principle "do good to others as God has done good to you," believers are asked to exemplify God's names in their lives. God is the most compassionate one, and humans are encouraged to have compassion for one another and for God's creation. God is the most generous one, and humans are encouraged to be generous. God is just, and humans are encouraged to stand for justice. God creates with wisdom and does not waste, and likewise, humans are encouraged to do the same in their affairs.

[22] Qur'an 7:19–25.
[23] *Sahih Muslim: kitab al-birr wa al-salah al-adaab, bab al-nahy 'an darb al-wajh.*

PART I GOD AND THE PROBLEM OF EVIL

In embodying God's name the Most Merciful One (al-Rahim), Abu Hamid al-Ghazali (d. 1111) wrote that believers should show mercy to the poor and provide them with whatever they need. In order to embody God's name the Peace and Source of Peace (al-Salaam), believers should not be prisoners of their anger and greed. Al-Salaam is the one whose essence is free from imperfection. To be the mirror of this name of God, believers should overcome such deficiencies. A Muslim is the one from whose tongue and hand believers are safe.[24]

Humankind remains at the center of Islamic theology because humans embody God's names (*asma al-husna*) in the most comprehensive way. They are also the ones who can read and contemplate the manifestation of these names in the universe better than any other creature. Humankind, therefore, carries a unique responsibility, which is to believe in God, to know and contemplate him, and to worship him. Departing from this responsibility is regarded as veiling God's signs (*kufr*); in other words, not reading the creation as it relates to God. A further step in *kufr* is *shirk*, which means to put other deities or humans on an equivalent footing with God. Islamic ontology is not limited to humans; it also includes supernatural beings such as angels.

Angels and Their Nature

When the time comes during the academic year to discuss the subject of angels, I always stop first to ask my students whether they believe in angels. A few inevitably affirm their belief, others will say they are agnostic, but the majority of the students respond in the negative. With modernity and progress in science, belief in supernatural beings such as angels is waning. While the number of those

---

[24] Abu Hamid al-Ghazali, *The Ninety-Nine Names of God*, trans. David Burrell and Nazih Daher (Cambridge: Islamic Texts Society, 1992), 54–55, 61.

who believe in the existence of angels is declining, the majority of Americans still believe angels are present. According to a 2016 study, 72 percent of Americans believe in the existence of angels; in 2001, 79 percent believed in angels.[25]

Belief in the existence of angels has been part of the teachings of many religious traditions, including Zoroastrianism, Judaism, and Christianity. Zoroastrianism, for example, recognizes several types of angels, each with a distinctive function. Followers of this tradition choose an angel for protection or an angel who serves as a guide to them. They dedicate prayers to that angel throughout their lives. In the Hebrew Bible, angels appeared to major figures such as Abraham, Moses, and Jacob. When Abraham was about to sacrifice his son Isaac, an angel appeared and stopped him. Abraham sacrificed a ram instead. In the Jewish sacred texts, angels are depicted in a variety of roles: healers, messengers, guardians or protectors, teachers, and warriors. Jewish scholars, including the medieval philosopher Maimonides (d. 1204), wrote of angelic hierarchies. Angels in each category have distinct features and functions.

Angels also appear frequently in the New Testament. One of the first mentions is in the Gospel of Luke when an angel appears to Zachariah in Jerusalem's temple. The angel brings the good news of the birth of John the Baptist.[26] In the same Gospel, the archangel Gabriel appears to the Virgin Mary and tells her she will miraculously conceive and give birth to a son who will be called Jesus.[27] The New Testament relates many other occasions of angelic appearances. As in the Jewish tradition, angels often appear as messengers, guardians, and teachers.

Probably no other religion emphasizes its belief in angels as much as Islam. Given that the Qur'an and the hadiths repeatedly

---

[25] "Religion," Gallup, accessed April 18, 2020, https://news.gallup.com/poll/1690/religion.aspx.

[26] Luke 1:11–20.

[27] Luke 1:26–32.

PART I GOD AND THE PROBLEM OF EVIL

refer to angels and that belief in angels is one of the articles of faith, not believing in angels calls into question the sincerity of a Muslim's faith. The Qur'an stresses that those who deny the existence of angels are misguided.[28]

Prominent Muslim scholar Al-Suyuti (d. 1505) compiled around 750 hadiths about angels in his work dedicated to their study in Islam.[29] Despite its importance in sacred texts as well as in the popular literature of Islam, the study of angels is often dismissed as unimportant.

Why Angels?

Since belief in angels is a key component of Islamic theology, Muslim theologians attempt to articulate reasons for their significance. One explanation is God's desire to be known through different manifestations of his creative activity. He revealed himself through the creation, of which angels are an important part. God creates beings who can observe his creation, contemplate its significance, and worship him as an expression of praise and gratitude. Following this line of thought, Islamic theologians argue that because God created humankind as beings capable of reflecting on his creation by virtue of their intellect, God could create other beings that could do so too. Creation as a whole is the manifestation of God's names. One of God's names is the Living One/the One Who Gives Life (al-Hayy). The manifestation of this name – of life itself – is present not only in the material world but also in other parts of the universe, including the spiritual.

If God is life, there is no nonexistence. Life is reflected to different degrees in both visible and invisible ways in every part of the cosmos. Angels are part of this living system. Since God is the

---

[28] Qur'an 4:136.

[29] For a study on Al-Suyuti's work on angels, see Stephen Burge, *Angels in Islam* (New York: Routledge, 2012).

hidden treasure and eternal life himself, he longs to be known and glorified endlessly. Due to many obstacles and distractions, humankind, however, is unable to worship and praise God ceaselessly and perfectly. For this reason, angelic beings respond to divine beauty and perfection in the most comprehensive way and fill the cosmic atmosphere with meaning, illuminating and making it "alive" in line with God's name.[30]

The Nature of Angels

What kinds of creatures are angels? What is their nature? The word for "angel" in Islamic theology is *malak* (pl. *malaik*). Angels are God's messengers. While God is not existentially in need of other beings, his majesty and sovereignty make it fitting that those beings exist. Angels mediate between God and humans. It is believed that angels are created from light (*noor*). Unlike humans, they do not eat or sleep, as these needs are not part of their nature. As in the Bible, the Qur'an recounts occasions when angels appeared to Abraham. On one occasion, he received four people as guests. Known for his generous hospitality, Abraham rushed home and returned with a roasted calf. He placed it in front of his guests. But Abraham noticed that they were not touching the food. Seeing that Abraham was concerned, the guests comforted him and gave him the good news of a son. Abraham came to realize that his visitors were angels.[31] So angels often appear in human form.

Angels constantly glorify and worship God. The Qur'an mentions that angels "never disobey God's commands to them, but do precisely what they are commanded."[32] In another verse, angels are described as those who submit to God and are free of arrogance.[33]

---

[30] Nursi, *Words*, 191.

[31] Qur'an 51:26–28.

[32] Qur'an 66:6.

[33] Qur'an 16:49.

PART I GOD AND THE PROBLEM OF EVIL

In this regard, there is no characterization of angels as either bad or fallen. Angels' lack of free will differentiates them from humans and places humankind on a higher level in the creational hierarchy: Humankind has a self or ego and therefore freedom of choice, while angels simply follow what they are ordained to do. In Islamic theology, angels have no gender. And while they are depicted as physical beings, even with wings, such descriptions are metaphors for their faculties or skills.[34]

The Role of Angels

Sacred texts of Islam not only refer to the existence of angels and their nature but also describe their roles and attributes. The four chief angels are the archangels Gabriel, Michael or Mikail, Azrael, and Israfil or Raphael. According to a hadith reported by the Prophet's wife Aisha, the Prophet would often recite the following prayer at night: "O Allah, Lord of Jibreel [Gabriel], Mikail and Israfil, Creator of heaven and earth, Knower of the unseen and the seen, You are the Judge of the matters in which Your servants differ; guide me with regard to disputed matters of truth by Your permission, for You guide whomever You will to the straight path."[35]

Gabriel is known as the angel of revelation. Because of the distance of God from humans, revelation to the prophets is received through Gabriel. The Qur'an mentions Gabriel as the one who brought the Qur'an down to Muhammad's heart with God's permission.[36] Gabriel would appear to the Prophet in diverse ways, including in human form. According to various hadiths, the archangel would often come to the Prophet in the form of one of his

---

[34] *Hadislerle Islam* (Istanbul: Diyanet İşleri Başkanlığı, 2014), 1:535.

[35] *Sahih Muslim: kitab salat al-masafirin wa qasriha, bab al-du'a' fi salat al-layl wa qiyamih.*

[36] Qur'an 2:97.

GOD, ANGELS, HUMANS, AND SATAN

handsome companions.[37] In the Qur'an, Gabriel also appears to Mary in the form of a man.[38]

While Michael or Mikail is God's messenger in charge of issues related to nature, Azrael is known as the angel of death. The Qur'an asserts, "The Angel of Death put in charge of you will take your souls, and then you will be returned to your Lord."[39] Death is part of God's own creation and design.[40] According to a story widely shared among Muslims, when Azrael was assigned to be the angel of death, he was concerned that people would hate him because of what he does. God answered that he would establish elements for death so people would not criticize Azrael as death's main source. Rather, they would think of the secondary causes as the reason for the loss of a loved one.[41] Finally, Israfil or Raphael is the angel in charge of eschatological signs who will blow the trumpet at the end of the world.[42]

The Qur'an mentions other angels as well. Among them are the *hafaza* angels, who are always present with humans, one on the left shoulder and one on the right. God assigns a *hafaza* to each individual to record all that person's deeds. Nothing a human says or does remains secret.[43] Considering that most crimes and injustices, including domestic violence and abuse, happen behind closed doors, the Qur'an warns the perpetrators of such crimes that eventually, everything will be unveiled. Islamic theology also mentions the angels of *munkar* and *nakir*. These angels question humans immediately after their death.[44]

---

[37] Muhammad b. 'Ismail al-Bukhari, *Sahih al-Bukhari: kitab fadail al-Qur'an, bab kayf nuzul al-wahy wa 'awwal ma nazal.*

[38] Qur'an 19:17.

[39] Qur'an 32:11.

[40] Qur'an 67:2.

[41] Said Nursi, *Şualar* (Istanbul: Söz, 2009), 342–43.

[42] *Hadislerle Islam*, 1:536.

[43] Qur'an 50:17–18.

[44] *Hadislerle Islam*, 1:536.

PART I GOD AND THE PROBLEM OF EVIL

Between Angels and Human Beings: Jinns

In addition to angels, Muslims believe in the existence of jinns: supernatural beings believed to be created from fire. According to Islamic sources, "Jinn, as psychic beings, unseen to most humans, occupy an intermediate state between the material realm of our physical experiences and the angelic and spiritual realms."[45]

God sent Muhammad as a prophet not only to humans but also to jinns. Human beings and jinns are mentioned together in twenty different verses in Muslim scripture. Not only does the Qur'an repeatedly mention jinns, one of its chapters is even named after them.[46] The chapter relates an occasion when a group of jinns sat with humans listening to the Prophet Muhammad recite the Qur'an. The jinns were awed by the divine words. The Mosque of the Jinn in Mecca takes its name from that event. The Qur'an also points to the prophet Solomon's relationship with the jinns in his service. Unlike angels, jinns can choose freely to become believers or disbelievers. In this regard, there can be good jinns and bad jinns.

Satan among the Jinns

Muslims believe that Satan is a jinn. The Qur'an refers to Satan as Iblis, the first jinn God created. Because of his piety and surrender to God, Iblis was initially part of a group of angels, though he was not an angel himself. According to the Qur'an, when God told the angels that he would create a human on earth, their concerned response was, "Will you place someone there who will cause harm and bloodshed, while we glorify you with praises and thanks?"[47] God responded, "I know what you do not know," and proceeded

---

[45] Joseph E. B. Lumbard, "Commentary on *Surat al-Jinn*," in Nasr et al., *Study Quran*, 1427.

[46] Qur'an 22:72.

[47] Qur'an 2:30.

GOD, ANGELS, HUMANS, AND SATAN

to create Adam, whom God taught his most beautiful names (*asma al-husna*).[48] He then asked the angels, including Satan, to prostrate before Adam. Everyone did so except Satan.[49]

When God asked Satan why he refused to obey, Satan reasoned that Adam was created from clay, while he was created from fire. Satan argued that he was superior to Adam and was therefore unwilling to prostrate before him. (For this reason, some Muslim scholars consider Satan to be the first bigot.) As a consequence, he was cursed and banished from heaven. Satan then made it his mission to tempt people away from the divine path. God granted him the freedom to do so while stressing that pious humans would be able to resist such deception.

Satan represents evil. However, neither jinns nor Satan has power over humans. In the Qur'an, Satan's tactics are described as weak.[50] Yet as noted in one of the hadiths, "Satan circulates inside the human similar to the blood in the veins."[51] He is always nearby and can have an influence on those who rely on him.[52]

Satan is not a power or entity in the universe independent of God's creative agency. Satan is a creature, not a creator. God gave him the freedom to test believers in this world.[53] But humans can spiritually and morally thrive through the temptations and challenges of Satan – and even rise to a higher level than angels.

Human Nature

The nature of angels and jinns can be clarified by contrasting it with Islamic theology's view of human nature. Humans were created

---

[48] Qur'an 2:31.
[49] Qur'an 2:34.
[50] Qur'an 4:76.
[51] *Sahih al-Bukhari: kitab al-ahkam, bab al-shadah takun 'inda al-hakim fi wilayat al-qada' aw qabl dhalik lilkhasm.*
[52] Qur'an 22:4.
[53] Qur'an 34:20–21.

PART I GOD AND THE PROBLEM OF EVIL

from clay and came into existence after they were equipped with a divine spirit. The Qur'an says that God first created humans from clay and fashioned their descendants from semen, an extract of humble fluid. He shaped them and breathed his spirit into them. He then gave them hearing, sight, and thought.[54] The exact nature of the spirit (*ruh*) is ultimately unknowable; humans have only a limited knowledge of it.[55]

The combination of both spirit and clay is known as soul. Once the spirit merges with the body, the human self (*nafs*) comes into existence. The soul tends to forget its nature and the reality that it "does not reside in the body but in the spirit and in God."[56] In this regard, the word *nafs* has a negative connotation in Islamic literature: "It refers to all the darkness within people that keeps them wandering in ignorance and distance from God."[57]

Unlike angels, humans are granted free will; they can choose to obey or disobey God, who is constantly testing them. The Qur'an mentions that humans were created with dignity "in the most beautiful state."[58] But because of their freedom of choice, they can also descend to "the lowest of the low."[59] Compared to angels and jinns, humans have more limitations due to their nature.

Islamic theology emphasizes human weakness. Being aware of one's inherent weakness leads to a full reliance on God and is an essential step toward becoming a servant of God, who is beyond all weakness. Recognition of human impotence is thus a fundamental means by which the believer is led to explore God's attributes – to come to know God as the almighty, the most merciful, and the most

---

[54] Qur'an 32:7–9.

[55] Qur'an 17:85.

[56] Murata Sachiko and William C. Chittick, *Vision of Islam* (Saint Paul, MN: Paragon House, 1994), 100–1.

[57] Sachiko and Chittick, 101.

[58] Qur'an 17:70; 95:4.

[59] Qur'an 95:5.

GOD, ANGELS, HUMANS, AND SATAN

generous.[60] Without understanding their own powerlessness, God remains unknown to humans.

Humans are mirrors of God's attributes, but they must be aware of their limits in relation to God. Awareness of these polar opposites – the unlimited weakness of humans and the unlimited power of God – provides insight into God's power, richness, and glory.[61] As part of their created nature, humans are dependent.[62] Being aware of this disposition brings one closer to God. Without the boundless spiritual poverty of humans, one cannot understand the boundless richness of God.[63]

The Qur'an and hadiths not only refer to humans' weakness and the fact that they are in need but also allude to their longing for eternity and attachment to wealth. The Qur'an points out that humans are often "excessive in their love of wealth" and think their possessions will help them live forever.[64] Therefore, the Qur'an repeatedly emphasizes that everything will perish except that which is turned toward God.[65] What is done according to the will of God can remain permanent. Humans are asked to be grateful for what they have been given. Being superior in the eyes of God is related not to wealth, rank, color, or race but to piety. Thus the superiority of humans to angels is a function of divine wisdom, not power or prestige.

As God created humans to choose freely to worship him, so he created angels and jinns to worship and glorify him by the necessity of their nature. Despite the fact that modernity and science have caused a decline in the belief in angels, this belief remains a key component of Islamic theology.

---

[60] Said Nursi, *Lem'alar* (Istanbul: Söz, 2009), 546.
[61] Said Nursi, *Mesnev-i Nuriye* (Istanbul: Söz, 2009), 152.
[62] Nursi, *Words*, 491.
[63] Nursi, *Lem'alar*, 39.
[64] Qur'an 100:8; 104:3.
[65] Qur'an 28:88.

PART I GOD AND THE PROBLEM OF EVIL

According to Islamic theology, God is the creator and the owner of the universe. The creation is the manifestation of his names. It reveals God's beauty, perfection, and power. God also created beings in the universe who can admire and appreciate his creations. Among them are angels, jinns, and humans. Their ideal response will lead them to love and worship God. The revelation of God's names in the world requires diversity in creation, which includes natural evil.

3 | Natural Evil and the Role of God

California had a record-breaking fire in 2020. By the end of the year, almost 4 percent of its land had burned. Experts highlighted a number of reasons for the devastating fire. Among them were drought and increased warming due to climate change. As a response to the fire and drought, a number of Muslim organizations in California – including Zaytuna College, the South Bay Islamic Association, the Evergreen Islamic Center, and the Islamic Center of Livermore – organized a prayer for rain. The person who was invited to give a sermon and offer a prayer was Hamza Yusuf Hanson, cofounder and president of Zaytuna College, the first accredited Muslim liberal arts college in the United States. In his sermon, Hanson highlighted that this world is a place of tribulations, difficulties, grief, and sorrow. Whatever comes from God is pure grace. People should respond to calamities with gratitude. God created humans to test them. But God also says in the Qur'an that if people turn to him with repentance (*tawba*), then God will send them what is good.[1] People sin, but when they face their sin's outcome, they don't take responsibility. Hanson made a reference to one of the principles that is often stressed in the Qur'an: "Each soul is accountable for what evil it commits, and no soul shall bear the burden of another."[2] He pointed out that the implication of this verse is in the hereafter. People suffer because of other people's irresponsibility in this world. God tests people collectively, and that is why innocents such

---

[1] Qur'an 4:17–18.
[2] Qur'an 6:164.

PART I GOD AND THE PROBLEM OF EVIL

as children and animals suffer during tribulations. However, these misfortunes are an opportunity to turn toward God with repentance and ask for forgiveness. Hanson concluded his sermon with prayer and a supplication of repentance.[3] A number of imams in California also organized a prayer for rain with their communities.

The Muslim community's response to the lack of rain in California is not a new tradition. It is part of a practice that dates to the Prophet Muhammad. In times of drought, Muhammad would often offer a prayer for rain (*salat al-istisqa*) and encourage his followers to do the same.[4] The implication of this prayer is that everything is in God's control, and he has power over nature. Therefore, God is the one who can send the rain. This approach to drought manifests an Islamic theological perspective on natural evil.

Natural evil remains a major challenge to the traditional view of God. Every day, about 150,000 people die. Among the leading causes of these deaths are cardiovascular diseases (48,742), cancers (26,181), respiratory diseases (10,724), and neonatal disorders (4,887).[5] In 2017, around 56 million people died. Approximately half of them were aged seventy years or older, 27 percent were aged fifty to sixty-nine years, 14 percent were aged fifteen to forty-nine years, only 1 percent were aged five to fourteen years, and around 10 percent were under the age of five.[6] In 2019, an estimated 5.2 million children under five years old died. Many of these deaths were due to birth complications.[7] According to some estimates, every year,

---

[3] "Turning to God in Tribulation," Muslim Community Center – MCC East Bay, YouTube video, posted September 25, 2020, www.youtube.com/watch?v=t-pukZSJk3c.

[4] Muhammad b. 'Isa al-Tirmidhi, *Jami' al-Tirmidhi: kitab abwab al-safar, bab ma ja'a fi salat al-istisqa.*

[5] Jenna Ross, "Global Deaths: This Is How COVID-19 Compares to Other Diseases," World Economic Forum, May 16, 2020, www.weforum.org/agenda/2020/05/how-many-people-die-each-day-covid-19-coronavirus.

[6] Hannah Ritchie, "What Do People Die From?," Our World in Data, February 14, 2018, https://ourworldindata.org/what-does-the-world-die-from.

[7] "Children: Improving Survival and Well-Being," World Health Organization, September 8, 2020, www.who.int/news-room/fact-sheets/detail/children-reducing-mortality.

nearly 300,000 women die in childbirth,[8] and around 60,000 people die because of natural disasters.[9] I should also mention animal suffering. For example, it is believed that over three billion animals were killed or displaced during Australia's devastating bushfires from June 2019 to February 2020. It was one of the worst wildlife disasters in modern history.[10]

These examples show that there is immense suffering that is associated with natural evil. According to Islamic theology, God is the sole creator and owner of the universe. There is nothing outside of his power and knowledge. He is merciful and compassionate. If this is the case, how do Muslim theologians reconcile natural evil with the existence of God? In this chapter, I explore their perspectives on natural evil and suffering.

The key term in Islamic literature concerning evil is *sharr*, and its opposite is *khayr* (good). As a term, *sharr* means something that is disliked, the spread of what is harmful, something that is incompatible with one's nature. The Qur'an employs the word in various ways. In some cases, *sharr* is described as what is impermissible and sinful. It also implies that people may not completely know what is evil and what is good.[11] The Qur'an uses other words that are associated with evil and suffering. Among them are trial (*musiba*), injustice (*zulm*), harm (*darra*), indecency (*fahsha*), misery (*shaqawa*), moral corruption (*fasad*), ill (*su'*), grief (*huzn*), sin (*sayyia*), and pain (*alam*). Muslim theologians offer a number of theodicies for natural evil. One of them is to emphasize God's power and full authority over creation.

---

[8] Liz Ford, "Why Do Women Still Die Giving Birth?," *Guardian*, September 24, 2018, www.theguardian.com/global-development/2018/sep/24/why-do-women-still-die-giving-birth.

[9] Hannah Ritchie and Max Roser, "Natural Disasters," Our World in Data, last updated November 2019, https://ourworldindata.org/natural-disasters.

[10] Daniel Vernick, "3 Billion Animals Harmed by Australia's Fires," WWF, July 28, 2020, www.worldwildlife.org/stories/3-billion-animals-harmed-by-australia-s-fires.

[11] Qur'an 2:216.

PART I GOD AND THE PROBLEM OF EVIL

God and the Creation of Natural Evil

The Qur'an points out that God is the creator and has power over everything: "Blessed is He in whose hands lies sovereignty, and he has power over all things. Everything in the heavens and earth belongs to God."[12] The Qur'an also mentions that God does what he wills:

> Say, "God, Owner of Sovereignty, You give sovereignty to whom you will, and You take sovereignty away from whom You will. You honor whom You will and You disgrace whom You will. All good is in Your hand. You have power over everything. You cause the night to pass into the day, and the day to pass into the night. You bring the living out of the dead and the dead out of the living; You provide for whoever You will without limit."[13]

In another verse, the Qur'an reads: "If God afflicts you with misfortune, no one can remove it but Him, and if He intends good for you, no one can repel His grace. He grants it to whom He pleases of His servants; and He is the Forgiving, the Merciful."[14] The Islamic scripture also implies that God is the creator of natural disasters such as drought, famine, and earthquakes: "We inflicted Pharaoh's people with famine and shortage of crops, so that they might take heed. No misfortune can happen, either in the earth or in yourselves, that was not set down in writing before We brought it into being, that is easy for God."[15]

The Mutazilites, a theological school that emphasizes reason (*'aql*), argue that justice is at the center of God's creation, including natural disasters. That is why the Mutazilites do not believe that there is evil in God's creation. Mutazilite scholars argue that God only creates what is the most useful and beneficial for the people

---

[12] Qur'an 67:1; 3:129.
[13] Qur'an 3:26–27.
[14] Qur'an 10:107.
[15] Qur'an 7:130 and 57:22.

58

(the doctrine of *al-aslah*). For them, in order to understand whether an act is evil or good, one must determine whether it is harmful or advantageous for people. God always creates with purpose, and there is no waste in his creation.[16] Otherwise, one may think that God is involved in unnecessary creation and indifferent to injustice. Therefore, the Mutazilites point out that it is incumbent on God (*aslah 'ala Allah*) to create with justice and purpose. For them, God is the creator of natural disasters and illnesses, but these things are not evil in reality. The creation of evil is inconsistent with God's justice.

Unlike the Mutazilites, the Asharites, a theological school that emphasizes the authority of revelation over reason, believe that God is not obligated to create with justice or according to the advantages of people. They highlight God's power (*qudrah*). The Ashari school, which became the mainstream school in the Sunni tradition, argues that everything belongs to God. God acts the way he wills, and one cannot seek wisdom in or benefit from God's actions. They support their points with passages from the Qur'an:

> Those who are wretched shall be in the Fire, they shall have therein groaning and wailing, remaining therein for as long as the heavens and the earth endure, unless your Lord wills otherwise. Surely, your Lord does whatever He wills. As for those who are blessed, they will be in Paradise, remaining therein for as long as the heavens and the earth endure, unless your Lord wills otherwise – a gift without an end.[17]

With these references, the Asharites point out that God's acts are not driven by what benefits people.

For the Asharites, natural evil and the suffering that results from it cannot be considered harmful or disadvantageous. In this situation, what matters is not people's perspective but rather how God sees it.

---

[16] Avni İlhan, "Aslah," in *İslam Ansiklopedisi* (Istanbul: TDV, 1991), 3:495.
[17] Qur'an 11:106–8.

PART I GOD AND THE PROBLEM OF EVIL

God is not obliged to create with wisdom, as this limits God's eternal power. To counter the Mutazilite position, Abu al-Hasan al-Ashari (d. 936) brought up the case of the three brothers (*al-ikhwah al-thalathah*) and their salvation in the hereafter. The first brother is Muslim, the second brother is an unbeliever, and the third brother died when he was a child. When asked what would become of the brothers when they died, the Mutazilite scholar Abu Ali al-Jubbai (d. 915) answered that the first brother would enter heaven and the second would go to hell. While the third brother would not be punished, he would not enter heaven either. Al-Ashari then asked what would happen if the third brother would say, "Oh God, if you would give me more life to live, I would have faith in you, obey you to enter heaven. You should have done what is the most useful for me." The Mutazilite scholar answered that God created what is the most appropriate for the child, because if he lived, he would rebel against God and would go to hell. Al-Ashari declared that this answer is unjust to the second brother, who died as an unbeliever, and inconsistent with God's justice. Because the second brother could ask, "Oh God, why did not you take my life when I was a child, I would not rebel against you and deserve to go to hell?"[18]

The Maturidi school offers a middle way concerning God's creation and natural evil. They emphasize God's wisdom (*hikmah*). There is nothing that is inappropriate and unnecessary in God's creation. Wisdom in the universe is the manifestation of God's name All Wise (al-Hakim). In this regard, there is no imperfection in God's creation. They still disagree with the Mutazilites' approach that God creates what is the most beneficial to people. The Maturidis contest that something that is considered evil (*fasad*) from our perspective might not be evil in God's wisdom. For example, God creates those who are disobedient to him and provides them with what they need. While this seems to be inconsistent with the doctrine of *al-aslah*, it might be compatible with God's wisdom.

---

[18] Mehmet Bulut, "Ihve-i Selase," in *İslam Ansiklopedisi* (Istanbul: TDV, 2000), 22:6.

NATURAL EVIL AND THE ROLE OF GOD

Therefore, God's justice cannot be held to the standard of people's reason and their understanding of justice. While we do not have the right to say that God is obligated to create with justice and according to what benefits people, we can say that God creates with wisdom. People may not be able to see the wisdom in God's creation, but it does not mean that there is no wisdom.

The Maturidis provided arguments against the doctrine of *al-aslah* from the Qur'an. First, a number of verses encourage believers to pray and seek refuge in God. For them, if one accepts the Mutazilites' position, then there is no need to pray, be thankful, and seek refuge in God. According to their view, God has already given people everything they need. If this is the case, people are seeking God's help for two reasons: to ask for something that they do not need or to hide a blessing that God already gave them. This is nothing but being ungrateful. Second, the Qur'an indicates that "God is the Protector of those who believe: He brings them out of the darkness and into the light. As for the disbelievers, their protectors are false gods who take them from the light into the darkness. Those are the inhabitants of the Fire, and there they will remain forever."[19] In this case, both believers and nonbelievers have the same conditions. However, God favors the believers and brings them out of the darkness. For the Maturidis, this verse contradicts the idea of *al-aslah*, because God should be an ally to the nonbelievers too. Third, the Qur'an points out that "those who disbelieve should not think that the time We give them is good for them. In fact, we give them time only that they may increase in sin, and there is a humiliating punishment for them."[20] Again, if the Mutazilites' position is correct, then God would not give more time to disbelievers to be more sinful, because this is not something that benefits them. Fourth, the Qur'an reads: "So let neither their wealth nor their children impress you. Through these God plans to punish them in this world, and

[19] Qur'an 2:257.
[20] Qur'an 3:178.

61

PART I GOD AND THE PROBLEM OF EVIL

that their souls should depart while they are disbelievers."[21] If God gives people only things that benefit them, how can one explain this verse? Because it implies that what God bestows on people is something that is working against them?[22]

Innocent Suffering

One of the challenges that the first two schools had to address was the suffering of innocents because of natural evil. For the Ashari school, while God will eventually reward those who die in the hereafter, they also believe that God does not have to do so. The reward is part of God's grace. Said Nursi (d. 1960), for example, points out that innocent people who die because of natural evil such as earthquakes will be considered martyrs, and their temporary life will turn into an eternal one. Their properties will be considered as charity (*sadaqa*) that will benefit them eternally.[23] There is divine mercy within their suffering. This world is a place of trial and examination. If the innocents were spared during natural disasters such as earthquakes, then everyone would turn to God. People would not have the opportunity to explore their spiritual and moral progress to the fullest extent. There would not be any difference between Abu Jahl and Abu Bakr. Abu Jahl is a figure who represents evil in Islamic literature because of his disobedience to God. He was the leading person who persecuted the Prophet Muhammad and his followers. Unlike Abu Jahl, Abu Bakr is known for his obedience to God and was one of the most loyal companions of the Prophet.

---

[21] Qur'an 9:55.

[22] For the Maturidis' criticism of the idea of *aslah*, see Hülya Alper, "Maturidi'nin Mutezile eleştirisi: Tanrı en iyiyi yaratmak zorunda mıdır?" *Kelam Araştırmaları* 11:1 (2013): 17–36.

[23] Nursi, *Sözler*, 243. For an in-depth study of Nursi's views on theodicy, see Tubanur Yesilhark Ozkan, *A Muslim Response to Evil: Said Nursi on the Theodicy* (Burlington, VT: Ashgate, 2015).

He is known for his goodness and generosity in the tradition.[24] Nursi turns to the Qur'an for this position: "Be mindful of a trial that will not affect only the wrongdoers among you."[25] In his interpretation of the same verse, al-Qurtubi (d. 1273) points to a hadith in which the Prophet uses the parable of a ship to explain the suffering of innocent people. On this ship, while some people are above deck, the others are below. If those on the lower deck in need of water would make a hole in the bottom of the ship instead of asking from those who are on the upper deck, the whole ship would sink. When people live in a community, "doing wrong and allowing wrong" will affect all members, both wrongdoers and innocents.[26]

The Mutazilites point out that there are lessons for people to learn from the innocents' suffering. While the innocents would be rewarded (*'iwad*) with eternal bliss, it is a test for their parents. The ideal response of the parents is to interpret the death of their children as ultimately good. Zayn al-Din ibn 'Ali ibn Ahmad ibn Muhammad (d. 1557) was a Mutazilite scholar of Twelver Shiism. He went through considerable suffering in his life. Among his sons, only one reached adulthood; another died in infancy. He also wrote a treatise on the death of his son. Like the scholars of the Mutazilite school, Zayn al-Din highlights the innocents' compensation in the hereafter. He also points out that there is even a reward for the suffering parents who lose their children. The children will, for example, intercede for their parents' salvation in the hereafter. The parents will be forgiven of their sins because of their suffering. In addition, the parents are not shamed and disappointed because of a child who grows up to have a sinful life. God tests his servants with loss so that they can learn to be patient and have the merits of an eternal life.[27]

---

[24] Nursi, 242.

[25] Qur'an 8:25.

[26] Caner K. Dagli, "Commentary on *Surat al-Anfal*," in Nasr et al., *Study Quran*, 489.

[27] Eric Linn Ormsby, "Two Epistles of Consolation: Al-Shahid al-Thani and Said Nursi on Theodicy," in *Theodicy and Justice in Modern Islamic Thought: The Case of Said Nursi*, ed. Ibrahim M. Abu-Rabi' (Burlington, VT: Ashgate, 2010), 152–53.

PART I GOD AND THE PROBLEM OF EVIL

Suffering for purification from sin and the merits of an eternal life are echoed in a number of hadiths. The Prophet, for example, says that even a minor thing, including the pricking of a thorn, will be compensated and that God will forgive or wipe out one's sin through suffering: "No fatigue, nor disease, nor sorrow, nor sadness, nor hurt, nor distress befalls a Muslim, even if it were the prick he receives from a thorn, but that God expiates some of his sins for that."[28] Aisha, one of the Prophet's wives, states that if a believer is very sinful and does not perform enough good deeds to wipe these sins out, then God will afflict the person with suffering in order to forgive their sin.[29] This approach is very similar to Jewish theologian Saadia Gaon's view. As mentioned in Chapter 1, Gaon explains that God inflicts those whom he loves with unmerited suffering in order to justify their eternal reward in the hereafter.[30]

Animal Suffering

Another pressing question that concerns Muslim theologians is the suffering of animals. In a number of hadiths, the Prophet Muhammad addresses animal suffering. It is also reported that Muhammad miraculously communicated with animals. In one case, a camel complained to the Prophet about being mistreated by its owner. Muhammad warned the owner and asked him to improve the situation of the camel. The Qur'an mentions that sentient beings will be resurrected on the day of judgment: "There is no creature living on the earth, nor a bird flying on its two wings, but they all are communities like you. We have missed nothing in the Book. Then to

[28] *Sahih al-Bukhari, Kitab al-Marda: bab ma ja'a fi kaffarat al-mardi.*

[29] Imam Khatib al-Tabrizi, *Mishkat al-Masabih: kitab al-Janaiz, bab 'iyad al-marid wa sawab al-marid.*

[30] Lenn E. Goodman, "Judaism and the Problem of Evil," in Meister and Moser, *Cambridge Companion*, 198–99.

64

NATURAL EVIL AND THE ROLE OF GOD

their Lord they will be gathered."[31] In line with this Qur'anic position, a hadith mentions that animals will be compensated for the suffering and injustice they experience: "On the Day of Arising, all of creation will be gathered together: the cattle, the riding-beasts, the birds, and every other thing, and it shall be by God's justice that He takes the hornless sheep's case against the horned one. Then He shall say, 'Be dust.'"[32] According to the Mutazilites, God has an "ethical obligation" to compensate animals for their suffering. For the Asharites, however, it is inappropriate to attribute "obligation" to God. For them, "God is expected to recompense animals for their innocent suffering but will do so out of His generosity and wisdom, not because universal moral axioms compel Him to do so."[33] Despite their disagreements, all theological schools believe that there will be compensation for the suffering of animals.

Natural Evil as the Manifestation of God's Names

As mentioned in Chapter 2, believers may know God through his names, which are manifested in his creation. The manifestation of God's names requires unlimited changes, transformations, and alterations in the universe that "necessitate death and extinction, decline and separation."[34] Natural disasters can be considered as part of the manifestations of God's names. According to Nursi, this world has three faces. The first face mirrors the divine names. Death, separation, and nonexistence cannot be part of this dimension, which reveals the names through transformation and change. The second face is related to the hereafter. Everything in this world

---

[31] Qur'an 6:38.
[32] Abu Hamid al-Ghazali, *The Remembrance of Death and the Afterlife*, trans. Timothy Winter (Cambridge: Islamic Texts Society, 1989), 200–1.
[33] Timothy Winter, "Islam and the Problem of Evil," in Meister and Moser, *Cambridge Companion*, 237.
[34] Said Nursi, *The Letters* (Istanbul: Sözler, 2004), 333.

PART I GOD AND THE PROBLEM OF EVIL

serves as a means for eternal life. From this perspective, death and separation will eventually lead to life and eternity. The third face looks to transient beings, including humans. People are attached to ephemeral beings. Their attachment may lead to pain and suffering. If people look at this dimension of the world from the perspective of the divine names, they will see that it also manifests life and eternity. Nursi concludes that transformation and renewal, including human and animal suffering, are manifestations of God's names.[35]

Evil Is the Privation of Good

Like many Christian theologians, Muslim scholars also point out that evil is the privation of good. Because God is perfect and beautiful, only good comes from him. The beings in the material world are limited because of their nature. Evil is the lack of good. It does not have a source, as God is the source of creation. Light, existence, and mercy come from God. Evil cannot come from him, as it is nonexistence.[36]

To make their point, these scholars classify the natural evil that exists in the world into two categories: essential evil (*sharr bidhdhāt*) and accidental evil (*sharr bil-ʿaraḍ*). Mulla Sadra (d. 1636), for example, argues that essential evil does not exist in the world, as it is the lack of good. Accidental evil is the result of creatures' relations with one another. For example, cold and warm are not evil in their nature; however, they can be harmful in relation to creation. Fruits may decay because of the temperature is inappropriate; however, that does not make cold and warm evil in nature. Another example is clouds. They are not evil in nature; however, if they block the sunlight, then they cause harm when a fruit tree cannot grow. Clouds may cause evil in relation to the sun.[37]

---

[35] Nursi, 337.

[36] Sedat Baran, "Molla Sadra'da Algısal Kötülük Bağlamında Şerr Problemi," *Şarkiyat İlmi Araştırmalar Dergisi* 11:1 (2019): 30.

[37] Baran, 18.

Goodness Dominates the World

Muslim scholars also state that evil that exists in the world is minor, and overall, goodness dominates the world. The Qur'an points out that God created everything with perfection.[38] The evil that exists is necessary and has benefits for creation. For this view, Ibn Sina (d. 1037) gives the example of fire. There is no doubt that the creation of fire is good and benefits people. However, when fire touches things, it may cause pain and suffering. This does not make fire evil, as the minor harm that is associated with fire is necessary for its creation.[39] In this regard, the existence of fire is far better than its nonexistence.

Concerning evil and goodness, the scholars also point out that one cannot abandon the greater good for the lesser evil. To support this point, al-Ghazali (d. 1111) gives the example of a cancerous hand. In order to keep the body healthy, one may justify the amputation of a cancerous hand. While the amputation may sound evil, there is a greater good behind it: keeping the body healthy.[40] A similar example comes from Nursi:

> A peahen lays one hundred eggs and they are worth five hundred kurush. If the hen sits on the hundred eggs and eighty go bad and twenty hatch into peacocks, can it be said that the loss was high and the affair, evil; that it was bad to put the broody hen on the eggs and an evil occurred? No, it was not thus, it was good. For the peacock species and egg family lost eighty eggs worth four hundred kurush, but gained twenty peacocks worth eighty liras.[41]

The point is that while eighty of the eggs were lost, incubation itself is not evil. The quantity is not relevant either. The gain is much higher compared to what is lost. The greater good cannot be abandoned for the lesser evil.

---

[38] Qur'an 32:7.

[39] Shams Inati, *The Problem of Evil: Ibn Sina's Theodicy* (New York: Global, 2000), 144.

[40] Al-Ghazali, *The Ninety-Nine Names of God*, 55.

[41] Nursi, *Letters*, 60–61. Kurush was the currency used by the Ottoman Empire until 1923.

PART I GOD AND THE PROBLEM OF EVIL

Evil Reveals What Is Good

Muslim scholars also underline that our notions of good and beauty will remain incomplete and static without evil. It is through evil and suffering that one can experience various degrees of goodness and beauty in the world. Good and evil often come together. For this view, Rumi (d. 1273) gives a number of examples: "Ruined the house for the sake of the golden treasure, and with that same treasure builds it better (than before); cut off the water and cleansed the river-bed, then caused drinking-water to flow in the river-bed; cleft the skin and drew out the iron point (of the arrow or spear) – then fresh skin grew over it (the wound)."[42] Rumi then concludes that the divine action is manifested in opposites and this is its nature.

Rumi gives other examples concerning the problem of evil. He notes that even if evil comes from God, still there is no imperfection in his creation. Creating evil is also part of God's perfection. To support his argument, Rumi describes a painter who created two pictures: one with a beautiful woman and the prophet Joseph and another with Satan. Both pictures reveal the painter's art. The evil in the picture also demonstrates the artist's skills. If painters are unable to draw evil things as well as good things, that shows a lack of talent. Rumi then states that evil and good in the universe are similar to this analogy. They are part of God's creation. Both illness and death are part of God's art.[43] Rumi also points out that there is no teacher without a student seeking knowledge. There is no doctor without a sick person seeking treatment. The existence of a doctor depends on the sickness of people. However, this does not mean that the doctor wills people's sickness or the teacher desires students' ignorance.[44]

---

[42] Jalaluddin Rumi, *Mathnawi*, book 1:307–10, trans. Reynold A. Nicholson (London: Cambridge University Press, 1926), 2:20.

[43] Jalaluddin Rumi, *Mathnawi*, book 2:2536–44, trans. Reynold A. Nicholson (London: Cambridge University Press, 1926), 2:352.

[44] Jalaluddin Rumi, *Fihi Ma Fih* [in Turkish], trans. M. Ülker Tarıkahya (Istanbul: Milli Eğitim Basımevi, 1985), 273–74.

Al-Ghazali offers similar reasoning: "As long as the imperfect is not created, the perfect will remain unknown. If beasts had not been created, the dignity of man would not be manifest. The perfect and the imperfect are correlated. Divine generosity and wisdom require the simultaneous creation of the perfect and the imperfect."[45]

The Best Possible World

The "this world is the best possible world" approach is another response to natural evil. In Islamic theology, this view was articulated by al-Ghazali. He argues that this is the best possible world created by God, and another possible world would be impossible (*laysa fi'l-imkan abda' mimma kan*).[46] Al-Ghazali maintains that even if all people's minds were put together and their intelligence was increased to the highest level, nothing would change in God's creation, as it is the best possible creation. They would eventually come to the conclusion that there is no injustice in God's creation because God creates with wisdom and measure. To support his view, al-Ghazali points to the measured creation even in the case of ordinary creatures: "Even if we wished to mention the marvels in a bedbug, an ant, a bee or a spider – for these are the tiniest animals – in the way they construct their dwellings, gather their food, consort with their mates and store provisions, ... we would be unable to do so."[47] He also illustrates the human body as the best form of creation. If we think of the way our eyes, nose, skin, and fingernails are created, the way they are placed on our body, their functions, and so on, there could not be a better possibility.[48] In the case of the eyes,

---

[45] Abu Hamid al-Ghazali, *Ihya' 'Ulum al-Din* (Cairo: Al-Quds, 2012), 4:399, cited in Eric Linn Ormsby, *Theodicy in Islamic Thought: The Dispute over al-Ghazali's Best of All Possible Worlds* (Princeton, NJ: Princeton University Press, 2014), 40.

[46] Al-Ghazali, *Ihya' 'Ulum al-Din*, 4:400.

[47] Ormsby, *Theodicy in Islamic Thought*, 46.

[48] Ormsby, 49–50.

PART I GOD AND THE PROBLEM OF EVIL

al-Ghazali wrote, "[God] placed the eye in the place in the body most fitting for it. Had He created it on the back of the head or on the leg or on the hand or on top of the head, it would be obvious what shortcoming would befall it, and what exposure to injuries."[49] Al-Ghazali then concludes that if there would be a better world, this would be against God's power and would be a sign of divine weakness.

Al-Ghazali's position is also supported by Ibn Arabi (d. 1240). Ibn Arabi reasons that the universe is the manifestation of God. The existence of the universe becomes a means of knowing God. Therefore, the universe is beautiful and perfect. It is the mirror of God's beauty and perfection.[50] Ibn Arabi also points to a hadith of the Prophet: "God is beautiful and he loves beauty." If God is beautiful, that means the reflection of his beauty, all creation, is also beautiful and perfect.[51]

Qutb al-Din al-Shirazi (d. 1311) also maintains al-Ghazali's position. He notes that if there were the possibility of creating a better world and God did not create it, that means God is not omniscient or omnipotent. The other possibility is that God is not generous. However, these attributes cannot be associated with God.[52]

In support of al-Ghazali's best possible world, some scholars also challenge the idea of a world with pure good or without evil. Mulla Sadra, for example, entertains the possibility with some counterarguments. In order to have a world without evil, Mulla Sadra offers the following options:

a. God would not create this world.
b. God would create the natural world with a nonmaterial nature.
c. God would create this world without the basic attributes.

For the first option to occur, God would forsake and abandon many goods. This itself is evil and inconsistent with God's generosity. For

---

[49] Ormsby, 49.
[50] Şahin Efil, "İbn Arabî'ye göre tasavvuf felsefesinde kötülük problemi ve teodise," *Felsefe Dünyası* 1:53 (2011): 94.
[51] Ormsby, *Theodicy in Islamic Thought*, 104.
[52] Baran, "Molla Sadra'da Algısal Kötülük," 24.

70

the second option to be true, the creatures would be part of a non-material world. In the case of the third option, God would create things without their natural attributes. For example, God would create fire, but it would not have its attribute of burning. This is not possible either.[53]

Al-Ghazali's idea has been criticized by a number of scholars. Their major criticism is that this position puts a limit on God. Al-Biqai (d. 1480), for example, points out that there is considerable suffering in this world. There are people who are born with disabilities; people can potentially hate and commit evils. How can one say there could not be a better world? God could create everyone as a prophet, and we could enjoy our heaven in this world in which there would be no death.[54] Another Muslim theologian, Ibn al-Munayyir (d. 1284), also challenges al-Ghazali's position. Concerning the best possible world, al-Munayyir points out that there are many people with disabilities. If the point of imperfections in this world is to know and understand what is perfect, God could just create one individual with imperfection, and this would be sufficient for us to understand God's perfection. However, the number of beings with imperfections exceeds the number of those with perfection.[55] Al-Ghazali's view was also criticized because it had some similarities with the Mutazilite doctrine of *al-aslah*.[56]

What Appears to Be Evil May Not Be Evil in Reality

Muslim scholars also discuss evil as something that may eventually turn out to be good even if people do not grasp it in the first place. In this context, the following verse of the Qur'an is often used as an argument: "It may be that you hate something while it is good for

---

[53] Baran, 27.
[54] Ormsby, *Theodicy in Islamic Thought*, 135–38.
[55] Ormsby, 200–1.
[56] Ormsby, 34.

PART I GOD AND THE PROBLEM OF EVIL

you, and it may be that you love something while it is evil for you."[57] Here the Qur'an lays out a principle: What is good cannot be based on what you like. What you like may turn out to be evil, and what you dislike might turn out to be good for you. This approach can be found in the Prophet Muhammad's life, as he often prayed, "Oh God, if it is good for my life in this world and the hereafter then bestow upon me."[58] Here the Prophet asks God not for what he likes or dislikes but rather what is eventually good for him.

Rumi mentions that creation cannot be based on our own desires or what we like or dislike. Depending on the context, what is poisonous for one might be a cure for another. He gives the example of a venomous snake. While venom is part of the snake's life, it is lethal for people. While for the animals living in the water, the sea is heaven, for the animals living outside of the sea, it is a form of suffering and death.[59]

Natural Evil as a Test and Warning for the People

Based on some of the verses from the Qur'an, Muslim scholars also look at natural evil as a test and warning from God. A number of verses are often cited to support this view:

> We shall certainly test you with fear and hunger, and loss of wealth, lives, and crops. But give good news to the patient, those who, when a misfortune befalls them, say, "We belong to God and to Him we shall return."[60]

> [God tests you to see] which of you is best in conduct.[61]

---

[57] Qur'an 2:216.

[58] Al-Bukhari, *al-Adab al-Mufrad: kitab al-du'a', bab al-du'a' 'ind al-istikhara.*

[59] Rumi, *Mathnawi*, book 4:65–70, trans. Reynold A. Nicholson (London: Cambridge University Press, 1930), 4:276.

[60] Qur'an 2:155–56.

[61] Qur'an 11:7.

[God] created death and life to test which of you is best in deeds.[62]

Every soul will taste death: We test you with evil and good, and to Us you will be returned.[63]

In the face of natural evil and suffering, Muslim scholars often emphasize this world as a place of test, not reward. The Qur'an also mentions that people will face trials and tribulations because of their sin and heedlessness: "Whatever misfortune befalls you, it is because of what your own hands have done, God pardons much."[64] In the Qur'an as in the Bible, this approach is best manifested in the stories of the prophets. Among them are Noah, Moses, and Hud. Their people are often punished through natural disasters as a result of their sin and disobedience.[65]

Spiritual Responses to Natural Evil

There is enormous pain and suffering associated with natural evil. In the face of natural evil, Islamic tradition underscores a number of spiritual responses. One of them is *tawakkul*: trust in divine providence. People going through suffering do everything in their power to overcome the consequences of natural evil and then put their trust in God. This spiritual response is often explained through one of the traditions. It is reported that the Prophet noticed that one of his companions was leaving his camel without tying it. When the Prophet asked him why he did not tie it, the companion answered that he put his trust in God. The Prophet responded that the man should first tie his camel, then put his trust in God.[66] *Tawakkul* is to believe that God is the creator and in control of everything.

---

[62] Qur'an 67:2.
[63] Qur'an 21:35.
[64] Qur'an 42:30.
[65] Qur'an 7:130.
[66] *Jami' al-Tirmidhi: kitab sifat al-qiyama.*

PART I GOD AND THE PROBLEM OF EVIL

In the midst of pain and suffering, the idea is to turn to God, as he loves when people ask for his help. The Qur'an points out that God answers the prayers of those who seek refuge in him with humility.[67]

Times of trials and tribulations due to evil and suffering are also times for worship and prayer. For example, the lack of rain is considered an opportunity to worship and pray to God.[68] That is why the prayer for rain does not simply ask God for rain; it is an occasion to turn to God. Nuh Ha Mim Keller points to this aspect of the trials as follows: "If not for the problems, fears, and pain man faces, he would remain turned away from the door of the divine generosity, and miss an enormous share of worship that benefits him in this world and the next."[69]

Another spiritual response is patience (*sabr*). The Quran often points out that patience is one of the traits of believers. It indicates that those who respond to suffering and evil with patience and turn to God will be rewarded.

In this chapter, I have demonstrated that while Muslim theologians have different approaches to natural evil and offer different theodicies, they all believe that God is the sole agent in the creation of natural evil. They highlight different attributes of God in relation to natural evil. The Islamic approach to evil and suffering is succinctly articulated by Erzurumlu İbrahim Hakkı (d. 1780), a Sufi poet and philosopher. I conclude this chapter with his lines:

> God turns evil into good
> Never think that He does otherwise
> The wise ones observe it
> Let's see then what God does
> Whatever God does, He does it beautifully

---

[67] Qur'an 40:60.

[68] Nursi, *Sözler*, 425.

[69] Nun Ha Mim Keller, *Sea without Shore: A Manuel of the Sufi Path* (Beltsville, MD: Amana, 2011), 372.

NATURAL EVIL AND THE ROLE OF GOD

Put your trust in God
Don't worry, leave it to Him
Be patient and accept it
Let's see then what God does
Whatever God does, He does it beautifully[70]

---

[70] Erzurumlu İbrahim Hakkı, *Marifetname* (Kahire: 1251H/1815), 385 (my translation).

4 | Moral Evil, Freedom, and Predestination

On February 10, 2015, Deah Barakat, his wife, Yusor Abu-Salha, and his sister-in-law, Razan Abu-Salha, were brutally murdered by a neighbor in their Chapel Hill, North Carolina home. All three were students and involved in charity work. Deah was a second-year student at the University of North Carolina (UNC) School of Dentistry. Yusor had just finished her degree at North Carolina State University (NCSU) and had been accepted to the same school as Deah. Razan was an undergraduate majoring in architecture at NCSU. Their families believed their children had been the victims of a hate crime and that the perpetrator was motivated by his animosity toward Muslims. In June 2019, the perpetrator pleaded guilty to three counts of first-degree murder and was sentenced to three consecutive life terms without the possibility of parole. While the families of the victims did everything in their power to bring the murderer to justice, they also found comfort in their faith. Deah's brother recited two verses from the Qur'an in his court statement:

> Do not say that those who are killed in the way of God are dead; they are alive, but you are unaware of it. Happy with what God has given them of His grace; and they feel pleased with the good news, about those left behind them who could not join them, that there shall be no fear for them nor shall they grieve.[1]

---

[1] Qur'an 2:154; 3:170. See "Farris Barakat (Deah's Brother) Court Sentencing Statement 6/12/2019," Our Three Winners Foundation, YouTube video, posted June 24, 2019, www.youtube.com/watch?v=YU-gU1BwX6w.

Deah's mother remarked that what had happened to her son was an ugly crime, but she also said:

> I believe that God is wise and He let this happen. I accept God's wisdom and I don't question it. I am sure there is some good for me coming out of [this tragedy]. I believe Deah did not die; only his state of being changed. He was among us, but now he is in heaven. Knowing that gives me a sense of relief.[2]

Echoing her brother and mother, Deah's sister pointed out that while nothing could make up for her family's loss, much good had come out of their tragedy. NCSU established a scholarship in their honor. The UNC School of Dentistry created an annual "Deah Day" dedicated to their memory. Every year on that day, the students of the school do community service to honor Deah's and Yusor's charity work. In addition, students raised $500,000 that created an endowment for a refugee project Deah and Yusor were working on.[3] This case exemplifies the Muslim understanding of predestination, good, moral evil, and suffering.

Perhaps no theological issue in the world's religions has been more contentious than the question of predestination and its relation to the role of God in human actions and to the problem of evil and suffering. God is known as all-powerful, all-knowing, and all-benevolent, especially in Judaism, Christianity, and Islam. If God predestines people to have certain fates, then how can they be accountable for their actions in this world and in the hereafter? If God is all-powerful, do humans have free will? If God is omniscient and already knows what people will do, how can they be tested by God? If God is all-benevolent, why does he not intervene, especially when innocent people face injustice

---

[2] For Deah Barakat's mother's remarks, see "Family of Deah Shaddy Barakat, One of Three Muslims Killed in Chapel Hill," Anadolu Agency, YouTube video, posted March 5, 2015, www.youtube.com/watch?v=3e9riCU9vpg&frags=pl%2Cwn.

[3] For Deah's sister's talk, see "Dr. Suzanne Barakat Addresses the Parliament in a Moving Keynote," Parliament of the World's Religions, YouTube video, posted December 6, 2016, www.youtube.com/watch?v=j9NlSUhO7OU&frags=pl%2Cwn.

PART I GOD AND THE PROBLEM OF EVIL

and suffering? Like members of other religious traditions, Muslims have also been dealing with these questions.

In this chapter, we explore predestination, freedom, and moral evil in Islamic theology. We first engage with some verses in the Qur'an and then look at different theological views concerning the notion of predestination. Finally, we explore the issue from the perspective of the divine names of God. The last section offers various ways of finding meaning in good and bad events. Before we turn to the notion of predestination in Islam, however, it is important to note that some Muslim scholars prefer the expression *measuring out*, as they believe this better captures the Islamic approach to human action in relation to God than the word *predestination*.[4]

Belief in predestination is the sixth and final article of faith in Islam. The tradition first establishes the other articles of faith and then builds the belief in predestination on them, as it is one of the most difficult areas in Islamic theology. In one of the hadiths, the Prophet emphasized not only the belief in "measuring out" but also "the good and the bad side of it." Human beings, as such, will experience good and evil in this world. However, they should always maintain faith that both good and evil come from God. Whether what reaches them is benefit or loss, they are to accept it with thankfulness and have hope in God's mercy.[5]

The two most common concepts that appear in Islamic theology in the context of predestination are *qadar* and *qada*. The word *qadar* (literally, "power") comes from the Arabic root *q-d-r*, which means "to decide," "measure out," or "judge." But as a term, it generally means that God knows everything in the past and future through his eternal knowledge. He is all-knowing, and nothing exists outside of his knowledge. The word *qada* means "to execute," "create," or "fulfill." Put simply, *qada* is the execution of *qadar*. According to *qadar*, God knows and has written down everything that will occur.

---

[4] Sachiko and Chittick, *Vision of Islam*, 104.
[5] Sachiko and Chittick, 113.

MORAL EVIL, FREEDOM, AND PREDESTINATION

Through *qada*, God creates and ordains what is in the *qadar*. Sometimes, these two concepts are used interchangeably. In emphasizing God's power over creation, phrases such as "Ma sha Allah" (what God wills), "In sha Allah" (God willing), and "La hawla wa la kuwwata illa billah" (there is no might nor power except in God) have become part of the daily language of Muslims around the world.

Measuring Out in the Qur'an

The Qur'an emphasizes that God creates with measure: "We have created all things in proportion and measure. We have treasures of everything. We send it down only in well-known measure."[6] The Qur'an also stresses that there is nothing outside of God's knowledge: "With Him are the keys of unseen: None but He knows them. He knows all that is in the land and sea. No leaf falls without His knowledge, nor is there a single grain in the darkness of the earth, or anything, fresh or dry, that is not written in a clear Record."[7] The prophet Abraham's supplication in the Qur'an depicts God's involvement in people's lives: "[God is] who created me. It is He who guides me; He who gives me food and drink; He who cures me when I am ill; He who will cause me to die and then bring me to life again."[8]

Theological Schools on Measuring Out

If God knows everything and is in control of everything, what role do humans play in their actions, whether good or bad? Islamic theological schools have taken three main positions on freedom and predestination.

[6] Qur'an 54:49; 15:21.
[7] Qur'an 6:59.
[8] Qur'an 26:78–81.

PART I GOD AND THE PROBLEM OF EVIL

First, based on various Qur'anic verses and hadiths, some Muslim theologians have argued that every human action is predetermined, and thus humans have no power over what they do. Human beings do not have free will either. Like leaves in a strong wind, they cannot control their actions. This approach was represented by a theological school known as Jabriya, whose first representative was Jahm bin Safwan (d. 745). In addition to believing that all human activities are predestined, adherents of this school argued that if humans were the creators of their movements, then they would be able to create in the same way as God. However, only God can create, and humans are only the products of creation. Among God's attributes is that he is all-knowing, and his knowledge is eternal. Everything then depends on his knowledge, and nothing can change.

The Jabriya approach had political implications, and it is therefore not surprising that others disagreed with this theological interpretation. Having the right answer for human actions in relation to God was important. In the civil wars during the Umayyad dynasty (661–750 CE), for example, many companions of the Prophet died at the hands of fellow Muslims. If human actions are foreordained, then believers must accept that Muslims who kill and are killed act as part of a plan foreordained by God. Other questions have revolved around what to make of the condition of someone who commits a major sin, especially a ruler. If humans are predestined to behave in a certain way and have no power over their actions, then believers should not revolt against the injustices of a ruler. Those who have argued in favor of this theological idea point to verses in the Qur'an to justify their positions:

> God is the Creator of all things and He is the Guardian over everything. God knows what every female carries and how much their wombs diminish or increase – everything with Him is measured. Whomever God guides is on the right path, and whomever God leads to stray is a loser. Yet you do not wish unless God wishes. God is full of knowledge and wisdom.[9]

[9] Qur'an 39:62; 13:8; 7:178; 76:30.

80

MORAL EVIL, FREEDOM, AND PREDESTINATION

When it was founded, the second school, Qadariya, disagreed with almost everything the Jabriya campaigned for. The Mutazilites later expanded on the Qadariya view, which emphasized human free will and power in relation to God. Unlike representatives of the Jabriya school, they argued that humans control their own actions, and their movements cannot be attributed to God. At the heart of this theological position is the question of justice in relation to God. Advocates of this school stress that humans are accountable because they enjoy freedom in their actions; they are the creators of what they do, whether good or bad, and they will eventually face punishment or reward for their choices. Attributing human acts to God is inconsistent with God's justice and incompatible with the idea of the world as a testing place for humans.

The Mutazilites argued that if human actions are predestined, as the Jabriya maintained, then human accountability would seem pointless, and belief in a day of judgment would be unnecessary. Predestination implies that God forces certain actions on his creation. This would contradict the idea that God is just. The Mutazila school's view of predestination has had political implications as well. According to their interpretation, rulers can be held accountable for their injustices, and their crimes and sins cannot be interpreted as divinely predestined. The Mutazila school was especially favored by the Abbasid dynasty (750–1258). Like the Jabriyas, they also justified their position through verses in the Qur'an: "Whoever does evil will be requited for it and will find no protector or helper apart from God. They said, 'Our Lord, we have wronged ourselves: if You do not forgive us and have mercy, we shall certainly be lost.' We showed him the way, whether he be grateful or ungrateful."[10]

A third position that offers a middle way was originally put forward by the Ashari and Maturidi, which later became the official theological schools of the Sunni, who today make up more than 80 percent of Muslims. The founders of both schools were initially

---

[10] Qur'an 4:123; 7:23; 76:3.

PART I GOD AND THE PROBLEM OF EVIL

members of the Mutazila school but later parted ways. They disagreed with the Mutazilites concerning their view of human actions. The Ashari and Maturidi explained their position through the doctrine of acquisition (*kasb*). While God was the creator of every action, humans were the ones who acquire them by choosing them of their free will. Therefore, humans are accountable for their actions. God wants humans to opt for good, but they have the freedom to choose evil. In this sense, humans are not the creators of their actions, but because they desire or wish for a particular action, God creates it.

The Asharite and Maturidi schools also distinguished between what is determined and what is known. In this regard, one should understand divine determining as a form of knowledge. According to Muslim scholar Colin Turner: "The knowledge of the knower depends on the thing which is known; the thing which is known is not, and cannot be, dependent on the knowledge of the knower." For advocates of these schools, therefore, people's actions are not determined according to God's knowledge. Rather, because God is all-knowing, he foresees people's will and choice. To elaborate this view, Turner provides the following example: "My knowledge that X is a thief is dependent on my having seen him steal, or on my having heard about his stealing from someone else; his being a thief is not, and cannot, be dependent on the fact that I know he has stolen something." Turner then points out that this person is "a thief regardless of whether I know he is a thief, and the fact that I know he is a thief has no effect whatsoever on his having become a thief, his being a thief now or the continuation of his thieving in the future." Likewise, Turner continues, what is known by God "does not depend for its existence on Divine knowledge: it is not God's knowledge of a thing which brings it into existence, or effects changes in its existential status, it is God's will in conjunction with His power." He concludes that:

> [C]ompulsion, therefore, is not something that can be predicated on knowledge, which is simply the awareness on the part of the

MORAL EVIL, FREEDOM, AND PREDESTINATION

knower of the thing which is known. Therefore, it is meaningless for anyone to assert that a man enters hell because God has always known that he would, in the same way that it is meaningless for me to assert that it is my knowledge that X is a thief that has made him steal from other people and end up in prison.[11]

In this sense, the Asharite and Maturidi schools differed from the Mutazilites by emphasizing that humans are not the creators of their actions – God is. They also differed from the Jabriyas by noting that humans have free will when they choose to opt for what is good or what is evil.

Muslim theologians often turn to the following story to understand the positions of each theological school concerning predestination, human action, and God. Let's imagine X fires a rifle, and because of this action, Y is wounded and dies. Here the question is raised: "Since Y's death was determined by God to be at such-and-such a time, what was the fault of the man who fired the rifle through his own choice? For if he had not fired it, Y would still have died."[12] In addition:

> If God had known from pre-eternity that X, whom He created, would enter hell, and if all things had been governed by divine determining, then the inescapable fact would have been that X had been 'destined' for hell from the outset. How, then, could X be said to have had free will, given that God knew before X was born that he would end up in hell?[13]

According to the Jabriya, even if X had not fired the gun, Y would still have died. They believed people are not the creators of their own actions. The Mutazilites maintained that if X had not fired the gun, Y would not have died because people are the creators of their

---

[11] Colin Turner, *The Qur'an Revealed: A Critical Analysis of Said Nursi's Epistles of Light* (Berlin: Gerlach, 2013), 375.

[12] Turner, 377.

[13] Turner, 375.

83

PART I GOD AND THE PROBLEM OF EVIL

own actions. The Asharites and Maturidis argued that if X had not fired the rifle, we do not know whether Y would have died or not.[14]

The Status of a Grave Sinner and Moral Evil

In the early years of Islam, Muslim theologians not only disagreed on the role of humans in their actions, they also argued about the fate of a believer who commits a mortal sin that is considered evil. Two major questions were at stake. What is grave sin (*kabira*)? What is the religious status of a grave sinner (*murtakib al-kabira*)?[15] While a consensus has not been reached on what is a mortal sin, some of the theologians maintained that an action that is clearly forbidden in Islam and requires punishment in this world as well as in the hereafter is viewed as a major sin. Among them are associating partners with God, theft, killing an innocent person, giving false testimony, and devouring the wealth of orphans.

The debate about the state of a grave sinner became an issue particularly during the civil wars following the death of Muhammad. A major event that sparked the controversy was the killing of Uthman bin Affan (r. 644–56), the third caliph and the Prophet's son-in-law.[16] Those who killed him justified their act based on the argument that he was a sinner. The killing of Uthman would eventually lead to civil wars in the early Muslim community. Many of the companions of Muhammad and the members of his immediate family died in these conflicts, including Ali ibn Abi Talib (r. 656–61), the Prophet's cousin and son-in-law, who succeeded Uthman as the third caliph, as well as his grandson, Husayn (d. 680). In the

---

[14] Turner, 375.

[15] For an introduction to the concept of sin in Islamic theology and the question of a grave sinner, see Vecihi Sönmez, "İslam İnancında Günah Kavramı," *İslami Araştırmalar Dergisi*, 28:1 (2017): 42–66 and Adil Bebek, "Kebire," in *İslam Ansiklopedisi* (Istanbul: TDV, 2022), 25:163–64.

[16] A. J. Wensinck, *The Muslim Creed: Its Genesis and Historical Development* (Cambridge: Cambridge University Press, 1932), 37.

MORAL EVIL, FREEDOM, AND PREDESTINATION

fight, both sides were Muslims. They killed and were killed. As such, what would be their religious status? Muslim theologians offered different answers to this question.

The first group, known as the Kharijites (literally, the ones who leave), maintained that if mortal sinners would not repent, they would be considered as unbelievers (*kafir*) in this world as well as in the hereafter. They supported their argument with the verses from the Qur'an. One of them reads as follows: "But those who disobey God and His Messenger and transgress His limits will be admitted by God to a Fire, where they will remain forever and suffer a humiliating punishment."[17] According to their understanding of the Qur'an, the Kharijites believed that a grave sinner should not be accepted as part of the Muslim community anymore.[18] Ali ibn Abi Talib was assassinated by a Kharijite with the accusation that he committed a grave sin by making an arbitration with his enemy during the second civil war. For them, Ali relied on his own opinion instead of relying on God's judgment alone.

The second group, known as the Murjiites (literally, those who postpone), differed from the Kharijites in their interpretation. They maintained that sin does not make a Muslim an unbeliever. The Qur'an mentions that God forgives all the sins except associating partners with him.[19] For them, the matter of whether a mortal sinner remains a believer must be deferred to God in the hereafter. God will reveal the final word about their fate on the Day of Judgment.[20]

The third group, the Mutazilites, offered an in-between position. They argued that the grave sinners are neither believers nor unbelievers. They will remain in an intermediate state (*al-manzila bayn al-manzilatayn*). If the grave sinners repent, they will become believers, otherwise they will die as unbelievers.

---

[17] Qur'an 4:14.
[18] Wensinck, *The Muslim Creed*, 47.
[19] Qur'an 4:48.
[20] Majid Khadduri, *The Islamic Conception of Justice* (Baltimore: The Johns Hopkins University Press, 1984), 28.

PART I GOD AND THE PROBLEM OF EVIL

The Maturidi and Asharite scholars took a more positive approach toward a grave sinner. They distinguished between faith (*iman*) and actions (*a'mal*). A person is in the state of faith when they believe that there is no god but God and the Prophet Muhammad is his messenger. Their actions, including murder, do not disqualify them from this state. In a number of verses, while the Qur'an offers retribution for Muslims involved in killing, it still refers to them as the believers. Their grave sin does not change their status as a believer.[21] Committing a grave sin is not because of a lack of faith; it is often about following one's selfish desires.[22] Also, the Qur'an mentions that every action is counted: "Whoever does an atom's weight of good will see it, and whoever does an atom's weight of evil will see it."[23] It also teaches that the believers should never lose hope in God's mercy even if they committed sin: "Say, '[God says], My servants who have transgressed against themselves, do not despair of God's mercy. Surely, God forgives all sins. He is truly the Most Forgiving, the Most Merciful."[24] The responsibility of a believer is to avoid sin and seek refuge in God, otherwise, as pointed by Nursi, a continuous sinful condition may eventually dismantle the light of faith: "Sin, penetrating to the heart, will blacken and darken it until it extinguishes the light of belief. Within each sin is a path leading to unbelief. Unless that sin is swiftly obliterated by seeking God's pardon, it will grow from a worm into a snake that gnaws on the heart."[25]

Predestination in Relation to Good and Evil

In Islam, predestination is often discussed in relation to the problem of evil and suffering. The Qur'an frequently refers to the evil, suffering, and calamities that people experience, all of which are

[21] Qur'an 2:178 and 49:9.
[22] Nursi, *The Flashes*, 112.
[23] Qur'an 99:7–8.
[24] Qur'an 39:53.
[25] Nursi, *The Flashes*, 22.

MORAL EVIL, FREEDOM, AND PREDESTINATION

part of their trial and examination in this world. Qur'an 90:4 explicitly states that humans were created in suffering. The word in Arabic that points to the suffering of people in this verse is *kabad*. According to some Qur'an commentaries, *kabad* pertains to hardship, suffering, pain, trial, and distress.[26] In other verses, the Qur'an specifies the forms of suffering and notes that God is testing people with "fear and hunger, and loss of wealth, lives, and crops."[27] The Qur'an also stresses human weakness and ignorance and indicates that because they possess inadequate knowledge, people cannot comprehend the wisdom behind their suffering and trials.[28] According to the Qur'an, people may dislike something while it is good for them or like something while it is bad for them.[29]

The Islamic theological position on moral evil and suffering in relation to humans is well captured in a number of narratives in the Qur'an. The story of the prophet Moses and an unidentified man known as Khidr in Islamic literature is one of them.[30] According to the Qur'an, God asked Moses who was the most knowledgeable among people. When Moses answered "Me," God revealed that there was a person more knowledgeable than Moses at the place where two seas met. He told Moses to go there and find the servant of God, Khidr. After Moses found Khidr, he asked if he could accompany Khidr in order to acquire his knowledge. Khidr replied, "You would not be able to be patient with me while traveling." When Moses assured him that he would be patient, Khidr responded, "How could you be patient in matters beyond your knowledge?"

---

[26] Abu 'Abdullah Muhammad al-Qurtubi, al-*Jami' al-Ahkam al-Qur'an* (Beirut: Muassas al-Resalah, 2006), 22:292. See also Muhammad Asad, *The Message of the Qur'an* (London: The Book Foundation, 2003), 1215.

[27] Qur'an 2:155.

[28] Qur'an 22:73; 33:72; 2:216.

[29] Qur'an 2:216.

[30] This story is narrated in chapter 18 of the Qur'an, "Sura al-Kahf."

PART I GOD AND THE PROBLEM OF EVIL

Humbled, Moses answered, "God willing, you will find me patient. I will not disobey you in any matter."[31]

They agreed to travel together, but Khidr again advised Moses, "If you follow me then, do not question anything I do before I mention it to you myself."

They set off for their venture. First, they took a boat. While on the boat, Khidr made a hole in it. Moses got frustrated and asked, "How could you make a hole in this boat? Do you want to drown its passengers? What a strange thing to do!" Khidr reminded him of their agreement that Moses needed to be patient. Moses apologized for his forgetfulness. Farther along in their journey, Khidr killed a young boy they encountered. Angrily, Moses said, "How could you kill an innocent person? He has not killed anyone! What a terrible thing you do."

Khidr replied, "Did I not tell you that you would never be able to bear with me patiently?"

Moses responded, "From now on, if I question anything you do, banish me from your company."

Their journey continued. Moses and Khidr arrived at a town and asked for food and hospitality from its inhabitants. They were refused. When Moses and Khidr were about to leave the town, they saw a ruined wall, and Khidr rebuilt it. Moses was disquieted and once again questioned Khidr's motives. At this point, they parted ways. But before they took their departures, Khidr revealed to Moses the wisdom behind his actions.

In the first case, the boat was owned by some needy people who, with their earnings, were feeding their families. In the direction the boat was moving, there was a king who was seizing all solid boats. He would not, however, seize a boat that had a hole. In the second case, the young boy Khidr had killed would in later life have become a criminal and committed many atrocities. In the third case, the wall was owned by two orphans in the town, and a treasure

[31] Qur'an 18:69.

88

MORAL EVIL, FREEDOM, AND PREDESTINATION

for them was buried underneath it. He built the wall so that when the orphans reached maturity, they would own it.

Obviously, the acts committed by Khidr seemed horrifying and immoral – full of suffering, fear, and concern. But the story reflects the Qur'an's approach to evil and suffering. In Moses, we see that humans are ignorant compared to God. Because their knowledge is limited, they are unable to understand the larger picture of the evil and suffering around them, reflecting the Qur'anic instruction: "What you see as evil might be good for you."[32]

Another account is the story of Joseph. Although the Qur'an describes the narrative as one of the best stories, it is full of pain and sorrow. Joseph faced moral evil at the hands of his fellow humans, including his own brothers. His siblings believed that their father loved Joseph more than them, and they became jealous of him. The brothers initially planned to kill Joseph so that their father, Jacob, would pay more attention to them. However, the brothers eventually modified their plan and threw Joseph into a pit. A caravan that was passing by found Joseph and took him with them to Egypt. He was then sold into slavery, and a ranking official bought him. Not long after, his master's wife fell in love with Joseph and attempted to seduce him. Joseph did not succumb to the temptation with God's help. However, he was still accused as the aggressor and imprisoned. In the prison, Joseph interpreted the dream of one of his fellow prisoners who worked for the king. Joseph's interpretation came to be true. The fellow prisoner was released and continued to work for the king. One day the king himself dreamed about "seven fat cows being eaten by seven lean ones; seven green ears of corn and [seven] others dry."[33] No one was able to offer a profound interpretation. The fellow prisoner remembered Joseph's ability to interpret dreams and told the king about him. The king then summoned Joseph and asked him to

---

[32] Qur'an 2:216.
[33] Qur'an 12:43.

89

PART I GOD AND THE PROBLEM OF EVIL

interpret his dream. Joseph informed the king that there would be seven years of abundance followed by seven years of famine. So the king should store up and prepare for the years of hardship. Not long after, Joseph was exonerated and became the chief minister for the king. Because of the measures that were taken prior to the famine, Joseph's brothers made their way to Egypt. The family was reunited. Joseph forgave his brothers for what they did to him. He said to them: "There is no reproach against you this day. God will forgive you. He is the Most Merciful of the merciful."[34]

In the story, while the Qur'an makes clear that it was the moral evils of fellow humans that made Joseph suffer, it also points out that God was aware of what Joseph was going through. Everything depends on God, and nothing is beyond his knowledge. Throughout the story, both Joseph and his father, Jacob, turn to God with patience, hope, and trust. Eventually, Joseph becomes a means of a greater good and remains grateful to God. Joseph responds to his brothers' evil with forgiveness and compassion.

The Qur'anic story of the creation of humans also provides an example of Islamic theology's perspective on moral evil. According to this account, God told the angels that he would create humans as successors on earth. The angels asked, "How can You put someone there who will do evil and shed blood, when we celebrate Your praise and proclaim Your holiness?" But God responded, "I know what you do not know."[35] God then created Adam and Eve in heaven, and they were expelled from there because of their disobedience. In their new dwelling, the earth, God equipped humans with free will, and they had the opportunity to reach their full potential. While God's desire for people is to use their capabilities for what is good, they also have the freedom to choose evil. God created humans despite their ability to commit moral evil. However, his wisdom justified their creation, including their evil acts, because of the greater good.

[34] Qur'an 12:92.
[35] Qur'an 2:30.

Moral Evil as the Manifestation of God's Names

As indicated in Chapter 3, evil and suffering are also related to the manifestation of God's names (*asma al-husna*). This world and the humans who live in it are limited in many ways, but they are unique configurations and manifestations of the divine names. To explain why God allows suffering, an analogy using fashion designers and models might be helpful. Once models are hired, they have no say in the clothes they will wear. It is a designer's right to try various styles on the model; a model cannot say, "I do not want to wear this dress." Let's imagine there is a beautiful designer dress that a fashion model likes. If the designer decides to try another dress on the model, she cannot decline it if she dislikes it. The designer can only produce and decide on the best dress after many tries on the hired model. These tests will eventually reveal the best of the designer as well as the model. Likewise, each creature can be considered God's fashion model. Without changes in our situation, including suffering because of moral evil, there is no way for people to know God.[36] It is through these alterations that one becomes acquainted with God's attributes, which are embodied in creation. For example, God is the Giver of Mercy (al-Rahim), the Most Generous (al-Karim), the Provider (al-Razzaq), and the Just (al-Adl). These names of God "require" the existence of the needy.[37] That God is generous and all providing has no meaning unless there are creatures who call on God to meet their needs, including when they are facing moral evil. People who suffer become the mirror of God's compassion, generosity, and justice not only in this world but also in the hereafter.

Fighting against Moral Evil

While Islamic theology emphasizes that there is nothing beyond God's knowledge and that moral evil is part of God's creation, it also

---

[36] Said Nursi, *Mektubat* (Istanbul: Söz, 2009), 271–72.
[37] Nursi, *Lem'alar*, 216.

PART I GOD AND THE PROBLEM OF EVIL

admonishes people to use their freedom to fight against moral evil and stand for justice: "O you who believe! Stand firmly for justice, as witnesses for God, even if it is against yourselves, your parents, or your relatives. Whether one is rich or poor, God can best take care of both. So do not follow your own desire, so that you can act justly. If you distort or turn away from justice, then surely God is aware of what you do."[38] In another verse, the Qur'an reads, "God enjoins justice, kindness, and generosity towards relatives and He forbids indecency, injustice, and aggression. He admonishes you so that you may take heed."[39] The Qur'an also points to some specific acts that people should avoid. Among them are theft, injustice, oppression, lying, slandering, and backbiting. The Qur'an repeatedly asks believers to support the rights of the most vulnerable in society, especially those who are unable to defend themselves. It also points out that it is an obligation upon the rich to share a certain percentage of their income with those who are in need. It encourages them to be charitable. Violating the rights of fellow humans will result in a severe punishment not only in this world but also in the hereafter.

In a number of hadiths, the Prophet Muhammad also taught his followers to stand for justice and be mindful of the rights of not only people but also animals and plants. Concerning an evil act, he said: "Whosoever of you sees an evil, let him change it with his hand; and if he is not able to do so, then [let him change it] with his tongue; and if he is not able to do so, then with his heart – and that is the weakest level of faith."[40] In another hadith, Muhammad said: "The best jihad is to speak the truth to a tyrannical ruler."[41] He did not want his people to be bystanders in the face of injustice and oppression.

Wrongdoers are asked to repent and seek the forgiveness of those they hurt because of their evil acts. The Qur'an also encourages those who are wronged to forgive: "But if you overlook their

[38] Qur'an 4:135.
[39] Qur'an 16:90.
[40] *Sahih Muslim: kitab al-Iman, bab al-bayan al-Islam.*
[41] *Sunan Abi Davud; kitab al-malahim, bab al-'amr wa al-nahy.*

92

offenses, forgive them, pardon them, then truly God is Forgiving, Merciful."[42] The Qur'an also points out that "the recompense of an evil is an evil like it. But whoever forgives and makes reconciliation, his reward is with God. Indeed, He does not love evildoers."[43]

Seeking Meaning in Evil and Suffering

Through suffering because of moral evil, humans progress and can move toward perfection. Without upsets, turbulence, and struggles, life is static and monotonous, and people cannot evolve morally, spiritually, and intellectually. Islamic theology teaches that pain may bring one closer to God and draws considerable attention to the suffering of the prophets as a result of moral evil, including Muhammad himself. Without poverty and hunger, we may not be able to appreciate wealth and surfeit. Without death, we cannot understand the importance of life. Without trials and tribulations, it would be difficult to imagine not only personal progress and gratitude but also material gains outside of one's self, such as in human rights and medicine. It is then appropriate to end this chapter with the observations of the great Tunisian poet Abu al-Qasim al-Shabbi (d. 1934):

> Reflect! The order of life
> Is a subtle, marvelous, unique order,
> For nothing but death endears life,
> And only the fear of tombs adorns it;
> Were it not for the misery of painful life,
> People would not grasp the meaning of happiness.
> Whomever the scowling of the dark does not terrify,
> Does not feel the bliss of the new morning.[44]

---

[42] Qur'an 64:14.
[43] Qur'an 42:40.
[44] Quoted in Ormsby, *Theodicy in Islamic Thought*, 265.

Part II | Human Nature and Suffering

5 | Aging, Loneliness, and Filial Piety

I briefly mentioned the story that led to the awakening of Siddhartha Gautama, who came to be known as the Buddha, in Chapter 1. According to the tradition, Siddhartha was born to a king. A wise man visited the king and told him that Siddhartha would be disinterested in worldly affairs and give up the kingdom of his father. Instead, Siddhartha would offer a path that would help people deal with their suffering and overcome their greed. Concerned that Siddhartha would not follow his legacy, the king took all the precautions to motivate his son to inherit the kingdom. He did everything in his power to expose Siddhartha to the worldly pleasures in the palace so that the son would not be distracted by the spiritual path.

However, being bored of the inside of the palace, one day Prince Siddhartha ventured out with his charioteer. On their way, they saw "a bent, toothless, and haggard" old man. The prince asked about the person, and the charioteer answered that old age is a stage of life that everyone goes through, including the prince and his family. Siddhartha responded: "So that is how old age destroys indiscriminately the memory, beauty and strength of all! And yet with such a sight before it the world goes on quite unperturbed. How can I delight to walk about in parks when my heart is full of fear of aging?"[1] On the second excursion, the prince saw a sick person and was disappointed to learn that many people often get sick.

---

[1] Philips Novak, *The World's Wisdom: Sacred Texts of the World's Religions* (New York: HarperOne, 1995), 52.

PART II HUMAN NATURE AND SUFFERING

He said: "This then is the calamity of disease, which afflicts people! … Since I have learnt of the danger of illness, my heart is repelled by pleasures and seems to shrink into itself."[2] During the third outing, Siddhartha saw a dead body on the roadside, and he was again distressed and puzzled by the people's heedlessness. It is difficult to have enjoyment in the world when everything is impermanent and life involves aging, sickness, and death. The prince then pointed out: "Yes, if this triad of old age, illness, and death did not exist, then all this loveliness would surely give me great pleasure. [But] the world looks to me as if ablaze with an all-consuming fire."[3] On the fourth excursion, the prince saw a monk who seemed to be content with his life. Inspired by the simplicity of the monk's life, Siddhartha left the palace behind and embarked on a spiritual journey that led him to become the Buddha, the awakened one. However, the goal of his mission was to find spiritual liberation by overcoming suffering.

This Buddhist story captures the Islamic theological approach toward human nature and suffering in many ways. Taking it as our departure point, the chapters in Part II discuss aging, sickness, and death in Islamic theology.

An Aging World

The aging population is growing almost in all countries. According to a study conducted in 2019, one in six people will be over age sixty-five by 2050, making up 16 percent of the world population. It was 9 percent in 2011. The percentage is higher in Europe and North America, where people over age sixty-five are anticipated to make up a quarter of their population by 2050. Another interesting demographic is that the population of people who are aged eighty

[2] Novak, 53.
[3] Novak, 53.

98

years or over is projected to grow significantly, from 143 million in 2019 to 426 million in 2050.[4]

This dynamic has generated unique challenges for the aging population. First, there are a number of diseases such as cancer, dementia, Parkinson's, osteoarthritis, and hypertension that are associated with old age. They cause pain and suffering. Perhaps no one described the situation in old age more candidly than Philip Roth (d. 2018), an American novelist: "Old age isn't a battle; old age is a massacre."[5] There is both physical and mental decline with old age. Some scholars consider aging itself as a disease and entertain the idea that it can be cured. Many universities and pharmaceutical companies are investing in research dealing with the problems that emerge in old age.

The second major problem among the elderly is loneliness. Individualism, the nuclear family, and scattered relatives increase loneliness among the older population. With the advance of age, many elderly people outlive their companions, including their spouses, friends, and relatives. A study conducted in 2018 reports that one in three US adults age forty-five and older are lonely.[6]

Every year, thousands of individuals over the age of sixty-five make appointments to see their doctors because of loneliness and isolation in the United Kingdom.[7] A study from 2017 found that over nine million adults are often or always lonely in the country. A number of researchers also found that fairly consistent levels of chronic loneliness are common among older people.[8] To address

---

[4] "World Population Aging 2019," United Nations, accessed February 22, 2022, www.un.org/en/development/desa/population/publications/pdf/ageing/WorldPopulationAgeing2019-Highlights.pdf.

[5] Philip Roth, *Everyman* (New York: Vintage, 2007), 156.

[6] David Frank, "1 in 3 U.S. Adults Are Lonely, Survey Shows," AARP, September 26, 2018, www.aarp.org/home-family/friends-family/info-2018/loneliness-survey.html.

[7] "Older People Visiting GPs Due to Loneliness," Age UK, November 15, 2013, www.ageuk.org.uk/latest-news/archive/older-people-visiting-gps-due-to-loneliness/.

[8] "Jo Cox Commission on Loneliness," Jo Cox Commission, accessed February 22, 2022, www.jocoxfoundation.org/loneliness_commission.

PART II HUMAN NATURE AND SUFFERING

the problem of loneliness, the United Kingdom established the Ministry of Loneliness in 2018. Japan also appointed its first minister of loneliness in 2021 to address the problem of isolation among its aging population. The appointment came after a spike in suicide rates. The period of old age becomes meaningless for many people because of the problems that they face. In 2013, a study was conducted with twenty-five elderly people living in the Netherlands. The participants point out that their lives are "completed and no longer worth living" and stress a number of reasons for their desire to end their lives: "a sense of aching loneliness, the pain of not mattering, the inability to express oneself, multidimensional tiredness, and a sense of aversion towards feared dependence."[9]

Humans are social creatures, and they love to be in relationships and known. Loneliness can be painful. It can even lead to many illnesses. The findings of a study suggest that "the influence of social relationships on the risk of death are comparable with well-established risk factors for mortality such as smoking and alcohol consumption and exceed the influence of other risk factors such as physical inactivity and obesity."[10] Some studies indicate that loneliness increases the risk of early death by 26 percent.[11]

Third, the idea of taking care of one's parents, or filial piety, is waning in many societies as it becomes more difficult to practice. For example, in China, where the teaching of filial piety is very much embedded in the culture because of Confucianism, it is nearly impossible for new generations to take care of the elderly because of their long life spans and the decline of the birth rate.

[9] Anne Goossensen et al., "Ready to Give Up on Life: The Lived Experience of Elderly People Who Feel Life Completed and No Longer Worth Living," *Social Science & Medicine* 138 (August 2015), www.sciencedirect.com/science/article/pii/S0277953615002889.

[10] J. Bradley Layton, Timothy B. Smith, and Julianne Holt-Lunstad, "Social Relationships and Mortality Risk: A Meta-analytic Review," *PLOS Medicine* 7:7 (2010), https://doi.org/10.1371/journal.pmed.1000316.

[11] Amy Sarah Marshal, "Early Depression Is on the Rise," *UVA Health*, May 31, 2019, https://blog.uvahealth.com/2019/05/31/elderly-depression/.

AGING, LONELINESS, AND FILIAL PIETY

For every young Chinese person, there are six elderly people to take care of.[12]

Given the realities and problems that are associated with old age in today's world, the question is, what should be the ethics of aging? As noted by Frits de Lange: "The existing ethical perspectives – whether they bear a Kantian, utilitarian, or eudaemonistic stamp – cannot stand up to a critical assessment: they all assume an individualist and activist understanding of the course of life and underestimate the moral impact of the fundamental relationality, dependence, and vulnerability of being (very) old."[13] So how should the questions of old age be addressed? In the following, I explore Islam's approach.

Old Age and Human Nature

A number of verses and hadiths relate to the nature of humans in old age. However, when is old age? Considering that the human life span has extended significantly in the last several decades, there are many answers to this question. It depends on a person's situation as well as cultural context. Many Qur'an commentators define old age as somewhere between seventy-five and ninety years old.[14]

Islamic tradition often emphasizes old age as a time of vulnerability. The Qur'an describes the last stage of life as one of weakness in a number of verses. With the advance of old age, humans experience physical and mental decline. If people's lives are extended, then their development or strength is reversed.[15] The Qur'an then invites believers to contemplate their weakness in old age, a stage that leads to their departure from this world through death. Old age is also a way to reflect on the resurrection. God first blessed people with

---

[12] Patti Waldmeir, "Escaping Confucian Disharmony," *Financial Times*, December 13, 2011, www.ft.com/content/a4042d52-24fd-11e1-8bf9-00144feabdc0.

[13] Frits de Lange, *Loving Later Life: An Ethics of Aging* (Grand Rapids, MI: Eerdmans, 2015), ix.

[14] Maria Massi Dakake, "Commentary on *Surat al-Nahl*," in Nasr et al., *Study Quran*, 676.

[15] Qur'an 36:68.

PART II HUMAN NATURE AND SUFFERING

strength in youth and then weakness in old age. He will then resurrect them.[16] The Qur'an relates the contemplation of the prophet Zachariah on the nature of old age as an example: "My Lord, my bones have weakened and my head is shining with white hair. Yet, my Lord, I have never been disappointed in my prayer to you."[17]

The Qur'an points to old age as a sign of God's power as well. It is the Creator who causes aging: "It is God who created you in the state of weakness, then after weakness gave you strength, then after strength gave you weakness and grey hair. He creates whatever He will, and He is the Knowing, the Powerful."[18] In another verse, the Qur'an reads, "God has created you and in time will cause you to die. Some of you will be brought back to the worst age, so that they will no longer know anything after having had knowledge. Surely, God is Knowing, Powerful."[19] Here the Qur'an indicates that it is not only the strength of people that wanes in old age but also their knowledge. God is the only one who is not subject to such decline.[20]

The scripture also mentions that with old age, unlike the common perception, people are more attached to life and what they own. In fact, wanting to live longer is part of human nature. Satan used humans' longing for eternity to deceive Adam and Eve. He told them that if they ate from the forbidden tree, they would live forever: "O Adam, shall I show you the tree of immortality and an imperishable kingdom?"[21] In other verses, the Qur'an reminds us that people tend to run away from death because of their love of life. However, death will still meet them, and they will be returned to their Creator.[22] People tend to forget their mortality. They constantly work for

[16] Jalal al-Din al-Mahalli and Jalal al-Din al-Suyuti, *Tafsir al-Jalalayn* (Beirut: Dar al-Qalam, 1983), 585.

[17] Quran 19:4.

[18] Qur'an 30:54.

[19] Qur'an 16:70.

[20] Dakake, "Commentary on *Surat al-Nahl*," 676.

[21] Qur'an 20:120.

[22] Qur'an 62:8.

102

this world as if they will never die: "Do you build fortresses because you hope to be immortal?"[23] According to a hadith tradition, when humans grow, two things will grow with them too: the love of what they own in this world and their desire to live longer.[24]

This sentiment of old age is concisely articulated in a story by Persian poet Saadi Shirazi (d. 1291) in his *Gulistan*. While having a conversation with the scholars in a mosque in Damascus, a person approached Saadi and the people in the gathering. He asked whether anyone spoke Persian among them. Saadi confirmed that he was able to speak the language. He was then taken to a man who was 150 years old. The man could only communicate in Persian and was about to die. They wanted to know the man's last wishes. When Saadi arrived at the bedside of the person, he was lamenting as follows:

> "I said let me say a few words I desire; alas the path of my
>   breath is stopped.
> Alas that at the table of good things of life I ate for only a
>   moment, before they said,
> 'Enough!'"

Saadi translated the man's words into Arabic for those who were around him. They all were astonished that the man "lived so long and was still regretful of leaving the world." Saadi asked the man, "How are you in this state?" The man replied, "What should I say, have you not seen what pain a person suffers when a tooth is pulled from his mouth? Compare that to the state at the moment life departs the body." Saadi then told the man that they could call a physician for treatment. The man lifted his eyes, laughed, and said: when the foundation of the house (i.e., the body) lost its balance and is in ruin, "neither determination nor treatment can have an effect."[25]

---

[23] Qur'an 26:129.

[24] *Sahih al-Bukhari: kitab al-riqaq, bab man balagh sittin sanah faqad a'dhar allah ilayhi fil'umur.*

[25] Shaykh Mushrifuddin Sa'di of Shiraz, *The Gulistan*, trans. Wheeler M. Thackston (Bethesda, MD: Ibex Publishers, 2008), 124–25.

PART II HUMAN NATURE AND SUFFERING

Perhaps, then, it is not surprising that today, so many are invested in meeting humans' desire for immortality. As Lydia S. Dugdale puts it in her *The Lost Art of Dying*: "Scientists and beauty experts alike are striving to find that elixir for infinite youth," now more than ever.[26] There are hundreds of scientific labs that are dedicated to aging. One can hardly find any scientific journal without articles on aging. Major leading academic centers, including Harvard, Oxford, and Stanford, have invested enormously in the question of aging.

While there are societies that venerate aging, our Western society "has a strong preference for youth and therefore, individually, for bodily interventions that preserve the appearance of youth."[27] According to a study released by the American Society of Plastic Surgeons, more than 17.7 million surgical and minimally invasive cosmetic procedures were performed in the United States in 2018. Americans spent more than $16.5 billion on these procedures. The number is increasing every year.[28]

Filial Piety and Islam

Many religious traditions teach filial piety to address the needs of the elderly, especially one's parents. Perhaps it is one of the most important teachings of Confucianism. The tradition identifies five criteria for filial piety. First, in their relations with their parents, children manifest the utmost reverence. Second, they aim to nourish them with utmost pleasure. Third, when the parents are ill, they

---

[26] L. S. Dugdale, *The Lost Art of Dying: Reviving Forgotten Wisdom* (New York: HarperOne, 2020), 28.

[27] Saul Levmore and Martha C. Nussbaum, "What Does It Mean to Age Well? Reflections on Wrinkles, Beauty and Disgust," *ABC*, February 4, 2019, www.abc.net .au/religion/our-aging-bodies-reflections-on-wrinkles-beauty-and-disgust/10214306.

[28] "New Plastic Surgery Statistics Reveal Trends toward Body Enhancement," American Society of Plastic Surgeons, March 11, 2019, www.plasticsurgery.org/news/press-releases/new-plastic-surgery-statistics-reveal-trends-toward-body-enhancement.

feel the greatest anxiety. Fourth, when the parents pass away, they mourn for them and demonstrate grief. Fifth, to demonstrate their sacrifice for them, they display the utmost solemnity. Once children meet these criteria, they fulfill their responsibility toward their parents. Filial piety is the foundation of every virtue and the source of moral teaching in Confucianism.[29]

Filial piety is also an important teaching of Judaism and Christianity, as honoring one's parents is one of the Ten Commandments in the Bible.[30] The idea of honoring could be rendered as fearing, revering, or respecting one's parents. In order to distinguish honor from fear, a rabbi gave the following example: "As for fear, I mean that a son may not stand where his father stands, sit where his father sits, contradict his father in speech, nor may he be on equal footing with his father. In contrast, honor means that a son must feed and clothe his father and assist him in leaving and coming home."[31] In the Bible, Jesus rebukes those who neglect their parents in the name of religion.[32] Right before his crucifixion, one of Jesus's major concerns was the care of his mother. He asked one of his disciples to take care of her.[33]

Filial conduct remains a key teaching of Islam as well. The following section of the Qur'an is often emphasized in this context: "Your Lord has commanded that you should worship none but Him, and to show kindness to your parents. If one of them or both of them reach old age with you, do not say to them a word of disrespect ('uff'), nor scold them, but speak to them kind words."[34] The scripture then

---

[29] Ching-Yuen Cheung, "The Problem of Evil in Confucianism," in Jerold D. Gort et al., *Probing the Depths*, 90.

[30] Exod. 20:12; Eph. 6:2–3.

[31] Quoted in Fu Youde and Wang Qiangwei, "A Comparison of Filial Piety in Ancient Judaism and Early Confucianism," trans. Noah Lipkowitz, *Journal of Chinese Humanities* 1:39 (2015): 284.

[32] Mark 7:9–13.

[33] John 19:25–27.

[34] Qur'an 17:23.

PART II HUMAN NATURE AND SUFFERING

reads: "And lower to them wing of humility out of mercy and say, 'My Lord, have mercy on them, as they raised me when I was a child.'"[35]

There are a number of principles that could be derived from this passage of the Qur'an. First, filial conduct is paired with worshiping God. Associating partners with God or worshiping anyone other than God is one of the most grievous sins in Islam. Stressing taking care of one's parents along with worshiping God demonstrates the significance of this teaching. There are a number of hadiths that support this instruction of the Qur'an. On one occasion, the Prophet raised a rhetorical question concerning major sins. He said that these sins are associating partners with God and being disrespectful to one's parents.[36] Pleasing God is connected to pleasing one's parents. Receiving God's wrath is connected to the reception of the anger of one's parents.[37] Filial conduct is often prioritized compared to other teachings of Islam. In one situation, a companion wanted to join the Muslim army for jihad. The Prophet asked him to take care of his parents instead. On another occasion, a man came to Muhammad and asked who deserved his respect and good treatment the most. The prophet answered: "Your mother." Then who the companion continued, and the Prophet again answered: "Your mother." The companion asked again, and the Prophet answered: "Your mother." When the person asked for the fourth time, the prophet answered: "Then your father."[38] Likely because at the time, women were believed to be more vulnerable and needed more protection compared to men, the Prophet emphasized honoring mothers over fathers.

The respect for one's parents continues even after their deaths. In one of the traditions from Muhammad, the responsibilities of children toward their parents are emphasized as follows: to pray for

[35] Qur'an 17:24.
[36] *Sahih al-Bukhari: kitab al-adab, bab 'uquq alwalidayn min al-kabair.*
[37] Al-Bukhari, *al-Adab al-Mufrad: kitab al-walidayn, bab qawlihi ta'ala, wa wassayna al-insan biwalidayhi husnan.*
[38] *Sahih al-Bukhari: kitab al-adab, bab man ahaqqu al-nas bihusn al-suhba.*

their goodness and ask God to forgive their parents, to fulfill their will (*wasiya*), and to continue to have friendships with their parents' friends as well as their relatives.[39] The Prophet also said that when people die, their deeds end except for three: ongoing charity, knowledge from which benefit is gained, and a righteous child who prays for them.[40]

Second, the Qur'an provides a standard for filial piety. When parents reach old age, the children should "say no word that shows impatience with them, and do not be harsh with them, but speak to them respectfully." To make it more specific, the Qur'an points out that children should not even say "Uff," an "expression of complaint and annoyance."[41] While fulfilling the needs of their parents, children should treat them with patience and tolerance. Some scholars suggest that with "Uff," the verse is "addressing the irritation a son or a daughter might feel in having to assist elderly parents with personal hygiene."[42] It has also been interpreted to "discourage the use of any kind of ugly, harsh, or dismissive expression with parents."[43] Islam teaches being good and respectful not only to one's parents but also to the people of old age in society. The Prophet said: "If young people respect an old person, God will prepare someone who would respect them in the same way when they are old."[44] In another hadith, the Prophet said: "A person who is not compassionate to those who are younger than them and is not respectful to those who are older than them is not from us."[45] Even during prayers, Muhammad asked his followers to be considerate of the elderly. He indicated that those who lead the five daily prayers should try to keep it light, meaning they should not

---

[39] Abu Dawud al-Sijistani, *Sunan Abi Davud: kitab al-adab, bab fi birr al-walidayn*.

[40] *Sunan Abi Davud: kitab al-wasaya, bab ma ja'a fi al-sadaqah 'an al-mayyit*.

[41] Maria Massi Dakake, "Commentary on *Surat al-Isra*'," in Nasr et al., *Study Quran*, 701.

[42] Dakake, 701.

[43] Dakake, 701.

[44] *Jami' al-Tirmidhi: kitab al-birr, bab ma ja'a fi ijlal al-kabir*.

[45] *Jami' al-Tirmidhi: kitab al-birr, bab ma ja'a fi ijlal al-kabir*.

PART II HUMAN NATURE AND SUFFERING

make the prayer long because among the congregation, there might be the weak, the elderly, and the sick. When the believers pray by themselves, then they can extend the prayers as much as they can.[46]

Third, the Qur'an reminds believers to remember their parents' favor as one of the reasons to honor them. The parents took care of their children; they raised them, and now it is the children's turn. In one verse, the Qur'an points to this reasoning as follows: "We have commanded people to be good to their parents: their mothers carried them through hardship upon hardship, and their weaning takes two years. So give thanks to Me and to your parents. To Me is the ultimate return."[47] In his interpretation of the Qur'anic approach to filial piety, Nursi points out that "the highest truth in this world is the compassion of parents towards their children, and the most elevated rights, their rights of respect in return for their compassion. For they sacrifice their lives with the utmost pleasure, spending them for the sake of their children's lives."[48] Nursi then continues that if the children did not lose their humanity, they would do everything in their power to honor their parents, to please them, and to make them happy.[49]

It is reported that a man came to Muhammad and told him that he carried his disabled old mother on his back for her to make the pilgrimage. He then asked: "Was I able to return what she did for me?" The Prophet responded that by this favor, the man could only return one of her breaths while she was pregnant with him.[50] As part of Islamic law, it is an obligation upon the children to meet the financial needs of their parents. Unlike in the modern law, the parents have a share of inheritance from their children.[51]

---

[46] *Sahih al-Bukhari: kitab al-adhan, bab idha salla linafsihi fayudawwil ma shaa.*

[47] Qur'an 31:14.

[48] Nursi, *Words*, 303.

[49] Nursi, 303.

[50] Quoted in Ibn Kathir, *Tafsir al-Qur'an al-'Azim*, ed. Sami bin Muhammad Salamah (Riyadh: Dar tayba lilnashr wa al-tawzi', 1999), 5:67.

[51] Qur'an 4:11.

108

Filial Conduct and Receiving God's Grace

Sacred texts of Islam often make a connection between filial conduct and receiving God's grace. The Qur'an, for example, refers to one of the traits of John the Baptist (Yahya) as someone who was kind to his parents.[52] Concerning God's grace, there is a story that is part of the hadith literature and widely known in Islamic culture. Three young people were in a mountainous area when it began to rain. They ran into a cave, but all of a sudden, a big rock fell from the mountain and sealed the mouth of the cave. One of them said: "We should turn to God and pray to him by mentioning the best deeds that they have done for his sake. Perhaps God will then remove the rock from the cave." One of them prayed: "Oh God, I had my old parents when my children were in their early age. I was herding sheep to take care of them. When I would get milk for them, I would first feed my parents." He continued: "One day, I was away, but when I came back, I saw my parents were sleeping. I brought the milk in a cup but did not want to wake them up. While my children were hungry, I did not want to give them the milk either because I wanted my parents to have it first. I waited for them for the whole night with the cup of milk." He concluded: "Oh God, I did it for your sake." The other two companions also mentioned their major deeds in prayer. Not long after, the rock was miraculously removed.[53]

In one of the hadiths, the Prophet states that if it were not for the vulnerable such as the elderly, children, and animals, people would not be saved from disasters.[54] The implication here is that the elderly are a blessing to society. People receive God's mercy and grace through them. In his writings, Nursi points out that he had a

---

[52] Qur'an 19:14, 32.

[53] *Sahih al-Bukhari: kitab al-buyu', bab idha ashtara shay'an lighayrihi bighayri idhnihi faradiya.*

[54] Abu Bakr Ahmad al-Bayhaqi, *Al-Sunan al-Kubra: kitab salat al-istisqa, bab istihbab al-siyam lilistisqa lima yarji.*

PART II HUMAN NATURE AND SUFFERING

student whose work was in order and he did not have any issue in his life. He later on learned that the student was good to his parents and was taking care of them.[55] The idea of being respectful and receiving God's grace is related to one's situation not only in this world but also in the hereafter. The Prophet said that one's parents can be the reason a person passes through the gate of heaven. Missing or having this opportunity is up to people's desires. Again, in the hadith, the salvation of people is connected to their treatment of their parents.[56] The Prophet said that heaven is underneath mothers' feet.[57]

Spiritual Responses to Aging

Islamic tradition offers a number of spiritual responses to the struggles of old age. First, given that most friends and relatives of an old person have left this world, old age can be seen as a stage of being with God and loved ones in the hereafter. Second, suffering during old age is considered worship, and people will be rewarded in the hereafter because of it.[58]

Third, old age is a sign of God's power. If people contemplate God and turn to him with gratitude and prayer, then they will be compensated. In this sense, Islam has a very positive image of old age and offers hope for the elderly. The Qur'an, for example, relates the story of Zachariah, who turned to God in prayer in his old age.[59] He asked God to give him an heir who could fulfill his legacy. Both Zachariah and his wife were of advanced age, and his wife was barren. Yet they were still blessed with a child, John the Baptist.[60] For those who feel

[55] Nursi, *Mektubat*, 272.
[56] *Jami' al-Tirmidhi: kitab al-birr, bab ma ja'a min al-fadl fi rida al-walidayn.*
[57] Nursi, *Mektubat*, 372.
[58] Said Nursi, *Flashes* (Istanbul: Sözler, 2007), 289.
[59] Qur'an 19:4.
[60] Qur'an 19:5.

AGING, LONELINESS, AND FILIAL PIETY

lonely and desperate in old age, they can think of God's compassion, generosity, and innumerable bounties manifested in the world.[61] Fourth, old age provides an opportunity for caregivers, including children, to reveal their compassion and generosity toward the elderly. It is also considered a form of worship for them as well as an opportunity to reflect on their own lives. Eventually, everyone will go through the same stage of life, and it is important for believers to contemplate aging for their spiritual progress. The following lines of the Ottoman mystic poet Niyazi Misri (d. 1694) illustrate such contemplation, with which I conclude this chapter:

> The sign of death is approaching, but the self is unaware,
> The parts of my body are shaking [aging], but the soul is
>   unaware.
>
> Every day a stone from the building of my life falls to the
>   ground;
> But the self remains heedless in sleep, unaware that the
>   building is in ruins!
>
> While my heart longs for immortality, God wills my death,
> I am suffering from an incurable illness, that even Luqman[62]
>   could not cure![63]

---

[61] Nursi, *Flashes*, 286.

[62] Luqman is mentioned in the Qur'an. He is described as a righteous man to whom God granted wisdom and knowledge. Chapter 31 of the Qur'an is named after him.

[63] Niyazi Misri, *Divan* (Istanbul: Emniyet Kütüphanesi Mehmed Rıza ve Şürekası, 1909), 25–26 (my translation).

6 | Illness and Healing

Sohaib Sultan served as the Muslim chaplain at Princeton University for more than a decade and touched the spiritual lives of many students as a scholar of Islam. In 2020, he was diagnosed with stage-four cancer and told that there was no cure for his disease. This was devastating news for him, his family, and the Muslim community. In one of his first reflections on his diagnosis, Sultan implied that while his illness was grievous and caused so much pain and suffering, it was God's decree: "He [God] gives and takes, He owes us nothing, all is His, His decree is merciful and wise and just even if we can't immediately see it."[1] In another post, Sultan pointed to cancer as his companion, one of the most important teachers in his life, a means of spiritual progress, and a reminder of his mortality:

> A deep awareness of mortality has taught me to be truly grateful and joyous for life's blessings. It has also pushed me to be where God commands me to be, and to avoid where God prohibits me to be physically, psychologically, and spiritually. And in this sense, cancer has cured me of certain outer ethical and inner spiritual ailments that I've carried with me for too long.

One of the most interesting points in his writing is when he refers to cancer as God's creation: "Cancer too is a creation of God's and He has so wisely decreed to place it in my body. I am not battling cancer. I am struggling with cancer and accepting that it has much

---

[1] Sohaib Sultan, "Accepting the Diagnosis," *Medium*, April 11, 2020, https://medium.com/@seekingilham/accepting-the-diagnosis-3685e22af2e9.

ILLNESS AND HEALING

to teach me in life's journey." In living with cancer, Sultan would often find comfort and clarity in this supplication (*du'a*): "There is no god except God, the One who has no partner. To God belong all the dominions, to God belong all praise, the One who gives and takes life, the One who has power over all things."[2] While Sultan's view of cancer is distinctive in many ways, it also reveals the Islamic theological view of illness.

Looking at illness through the lens of religion is an ancient approach. In Hinduism, illness is associated with one's karma. Hindus often turn to a deity for their mental and physical well-being. One can observe similar approaches in Buddhism as well. Like in Hinduism, illness is associated with karma. Therefore, the followers of the Buddha often seek to change their karma through meritorious deeds in order to have a better state of health in the future. The Buddha is believed to be a supreme physician. His teachings can cure the illnesses of those who practice his teachings.[3]

In Judaism, God is known to be omnipotent and omniscient. In the Hebrew Bible, illness is often mentioned as an affliction from God, and he is the one who eventually restores his people's health. One example is the story of Job, who was afflicted with sickness by God and eventually healed because of his devotion to and trust in God.

God as the healer is also a common theme in the New Testament. It relates the miracles of Jesus healing both mental and physical illnesses. In one case, Jesus went to a town and cured all the people who had certain sicknesses.[4] In another instance, a blind man came to Jesus. Jesus made some mud and smeared it on the face of the man.

---

[2] Sohaib Sultan, "Life Lessons: Living with Cancer," *Medium*, January 9, 2021, https://medium.com/@seekingilham/life-lessons-living-with-cancer-49940fbd3754.

[3] Edward Canda et al., "World Religious Views of Health and Healing," University of Kansas, Spiritual Diversity and Social Work Initiative, accessed February 1, 2022, https://spiritualdiversity.ku.edu/sites/spiritualitydiversity.drupal.ku.edu/files/docs/Health/World%20Religious%20Views%20of%20Health%20and%20Healing.pdf.

[4] Matt. 9:35.

PART II HUMAN NATURE AND SUFFERING

He then asked the man to go and wash his face with water. When the man cleaned the mud from his face, he had his sight back.[5] A woman who had bleeding for twelve years came to Jesus and touched his cloak. Jesus told her: "Don't worry, you are now well because of your faith."[6] The woman then was miraculously healed.

Jesus also encouraged his disciples to go out and cure the sick. He is known to be a physician in the catechism of the Roman Catholic Church.[7] One of the sacraments in the Catholic tradition, for example, is the anointing of the sick. According to the catechism:

> When the Sacrament of Anointing of the Sick is given, the hoped-for effect is that, if it be God's will, the person be physically healed of illness. But even if there is no physical healing, the primary effect of the Sacrament is a spiritual healing by which the sick person receives the Holy Spirit's gift of peace and courage to deal with the difficulties that accompany serious illness or the frailty of old age.[8]

The idea is that one can find both spiritual and physical healing through this ritual.

Today, an increasing number of mainstream churches and synagogues hold "healing services" and "healing circles" in the United States.[9] According to a study published in 2016, more than 75 percent of Americans have relied on healing prayer at some point in their lives. The percentage of praying for others was even higher.[10] Many of them have the conviction that God can cure someone, even if science

---

[5] John 9:6–7.

[6] Matt. 9:20–22.

[7] "Catechism of the Catholic Church: The Anointing of the Sick," Holy See, accessed February 4, 2022, www.vatican.va/archive/ccc_css/archive/catechism/p2s2c2a5.htm.

[8] "Anointing of the Sick," United States Conference of Catholic Bishops, accessed February 6, 2022, www.usccb.org/prayer-and-worship/sacraments-and-sacramentals/anointing-of-the-sick.

[9] For a study, see Linda L. Barnes and Susan S. Sered, eds., *Religion and Healing in America* (Oxford: Oxford University Press, 2005).

[10] Jeff Levin, "Prevalence and Religious Predictors of Healing Prayer Use in the USA: Findings from the Baylor Religion Survey," *Journal of Religion and Health* 55 (2016): 1136–58.

says the person has an incurable disease. They turn to prayer as healing alongside medical care. Many modern doctors incorporate this approach in the treatment of their patients. The Cleveland Clinic, one of the best hospitals in the United States, for example, provides a number of healing services. One of them is spiritual support from clinically trained chaplains of different faiths.[11] Many hospitals in the United States offer a similar service to their patients.

Illness as the Creation of God

Like the followers of other religious traditions, Muslims also turn to God and their religion to understand illness and find comfort. Perhaps one of the most distinctive teachings of Islam concerning illness is the belief that it is created by God. A disease can only inflict a person with God's permission. While there is much pain and suffering that is associated with illness, it is not considered evil. Illness not only demonstrates God's power over humans; it also manifests their weakness in relation to the Creator. Illness is often presented as a trial in the tradition. God tests his servants through afflictions.

God as the Healer (al-Shafi)

God is not only the creator of the illness; he is also the healer. One of God's names in Islam is the Healer (al-Shafi). God is the one who can cure physical, mental, and spiritual illnesses. In the Qur'an, when Abraham challenges those who do not believe in one God, he describes the God whom he worships as follows: God is the creator, the provider, and the healer.[12]

---

[11] The Cleveland Clinics in the United States offers healing services to its patients. See "Healing Services," Cleveland Clinic, accessed February 5, 2022, https://my.clevelandclinic.org/departments/patient-experience/depts/spiritual-care/healing-services.

[12] Qur'an 26:78–80.

PART II HUMAN NATURE AND SUFFERING

God as a healer is also mentioned in a number of hadiths. Muhammad's wife Aisha reported that when anyone in the Prophet's circle had an illness, he would rub the area of the pain and recite this prayer for healing: "O God, Lord of people, relieve me from my suffering. Heal me as You are the only Healer and there is no cure except the one that comes from You. It is your cure that dismantles illness completely."[13] On another occasion, one of Muhammad's companions complained about a pain in his body. The Prophet then asked the companion to place his hand where he was feeling the pain and say "in the name of God (Bismillah) three times and invoke this phrase seven times: I seek refuge in God and his power from the suffering that has inflicted me."[14]

The Prophet himself suffered immensely from illness. His wife Aisha reported, "I never saw anybody suffering so much from sickness as God's messenger."[15] Muhammad would often turn to God with the following prayer during his illness: "O God, forgive me, bestow Your mercy on me, and include me among the companions who are elevated."[16]

Muhammad as a Means of Healing

Muhammad is often viewed as a means of healing in Islamic tradition. It is reported in a number of hadiths that, like Jesus, he miraculously cured those who came to him for healing. For example, when the Prophet's wives became sick, he would place his hand over the spot of their pain and invoke this prayer over them: "O Lord of the people! Remove the difficulty and bring about healing as You are the Healer.

---

[13] *Sahih Muslim: kitab al-salam, bab istihbab ruqyah al-marid.*

[14] *Sahih Muslim: kitab al-salam, bab istihbab wad' yadihi 'ala mawdi' al-'alam ma'a al-du'a'.*

[15] *Sahih al-Bukhari: kitab al-marda, bab shidda al-marda.*

[16] *Sahih al-Bukhari: kitab al-marda, bab tamanna al-marid al-mawt.*

ILLNESS AND HEALING

There is no healing but Your Healing, a healing that will leave no ailment."[17]

The followers of Muhammad even sought his blessings for healing after his death. Imam Busiri of Egypt, a thirteenth-century Sufi and poet, for example, was afflicted with paralysis. He persistently sought healing from God through worship and prayers. Busiri also wrote a number of poems in praise of Muhammad. One night, the Prophet appeared in his dream and asked him to recite one of his poems. Busiri was not sure which one to deliver, as he had many poems in praise of the Prophet. Muhammad then read out loud the first lines of one of them, and Busiri started to narrate it while the Prophet was listening. When Busiri finished reciting the poem, the Prophet took off his cloak and covered Busiri's body with it. He then patted the paralyzed area of his body. When Busiri got up in the morning, he realized that he was cured of his paralysis. The story became public, and the poem is known as the poem of the cloak or mantle (*qasida al-burda*). The poem is widely recited by Muslims as a form of remembering God and a means of healing for those who have paralysis.[18] There are also a number of hadiths in which Muhammad asked his followers to seek medical assistance. In one of them, he said: "Seek medical treatment because God has not sent down a disease without sending down remedy for it."[19] The Prophet also taught a number of treatment methods, including consuming honey and blackseed. He also recommended the use of wet cupping (*hijama*), a suction method to draw blood out of the body. Muhammad's reports regarding treatments are collected under the title "prophetic medicine" (*tibb al-nabawi*), and many Muslims use them as references in addition to modern medicine.[20]

---

[17] *Sahih al-Bukhari: kitab al-tib, bab mash al-raqi al-waj' bi yadih al-yumna.*

[18] Mahmut Kaya, "Kasidetü'l Bürde," in *İslam Ansiklopedisi* (Istanbul: TDV, 2001), 24:568–69.

[19] *Sunan Abi Davud: kitab al-tibb, bab fi al-rajul yatadawa.*

[20] Many hadith collections, including *Sahih al-Bukhari, Sunan Abi Davud* and *Jami' al-Tirmidhi*, have a chapter on prophetic medicine (*kitab al-tibb*). Also see Ibn

PART II HUMAN NATURE AND SUFFERING

The Qur'an as a Source of Healing

Muslims also turn to their scripture for healing. The healing aspect of the divine words is highlighted in a number of verses in the Qur'an:

> People, there has come to you an advice from your Lord, a healing for what is in the hearts, and a guidance and a mercy for the believers.[21]
>
> We send down the Quran as healing and mercy for the believer, but it increases the wrongdoers only in loss.[22]
>
> It [the Qur'an] is guidance and healing for those who have faith.[23]

Because of the healing aspect of the Qur'an, Muhammad repeatedly encouraged his followers to seek healing from the scripture. The Prophet's wife Aisha reported that "whenever the Prophet became sick, he would recite Surat Al-Falaq and Surat Al-Nas [chapters 113–14] and then blow his breath over his body. When he became seriously ill, I used to recite these two chapters of the Qur'an and rub his hands over his body hoping for their blessings."[24]

Following the example of the Prophet, Muslims have been using the Qur'anic verses for both spiritual and physical sickness.

Illness as a Means of Spiritual Progress

Illness is also often seen as a means of spiritual progress. People who are sick can be more mindful of the nature of themselves and this world. This aspect of illness is stressed in a number of hadiths. Muhammad said: "When God wants to do good to somebody, He

---

Qayyim al-Jawziyya, *al-Tibb al-Nabawi*, ed. Muhammad Fathi Abu Bakr (Cairo: al-Dar al-Misriyya al-Lubnaniyya, 1989).

[21] Qur'an 10:57.

[22] Qur'an 17:82.

[23] Qur'an 41:44.

[24] *Sahih al-Bukhari: kitab fadail al-qur'an, bab fadl al-mu'awwidhat.*

ILLNESS AND HEALING

afflicts them with trials."[25] God inflicts those whom he loves with illness so that they can earn merits and progress spiritually. In another hadith, the Prophet pointed out that "one night's pain and sickness is better than forty years of worship."[26] So illness is a form of worship and plays a key role in one's spiritual well-being. People should be thankful and grateful to God not only in times of prosperity but also in times of struggle. God wipes out the believers' sin, purifying them for their spiritual progress through suffering. A tradition reads: "God wipes out the believers' sin through the misfortunes that befall upon them even if it is the prick of a thorn."[27]

Rumi, for example, points out that sickness can be a means of remembering God, and that is why people should be thankful for their sickness. For him, "pain is a treasure, for there are mercies in it." Fever, suffering, and sleeplessness because of sickness are blessings. Illness during old age is a sign of God's compassion and generosity: "He too had given me pain in the back, so that every midnight I cannot help springing up quickly from sleep. In order that I may not slumber all night like a buffalo, God of His grace has given me pains."[28] Rumi writes that his soul found sweetness in bitterness that come from God, and he fell in love with his pain and grief because it was pleasing to his Creator.[29]

Rumi also mentions that illness gives humans an opportunity to repent of their sins and turn to God. In the midst of their illness, they see the ugliness of their sin and intend to do better. Sickness may make people more thoughtful and humble. Suffering because of physical sickness is a channel to spiritual advancement.[30]

---

[25] *Sahih al-Bukhari: kitab al-marda, bab ma ja'a fi kaffarah al-marad.*
[26] *Sahih al-Bukhari: kitab al-marda, bab ma ja'a fi kaffarah al-marad.*
[27] *Sahih al-Bukhari: kitab al-marda, bab ma ja'a fi kaffarah al-marad.*
[28] Rumi, *Mathnawi*, book 2:2255–60, trans. Reynold A. Nicholson (London: Cambridge University Press, 1926), 2:338.
[29] Rumi, *Mathnawi*, book 1:1777–78, trans. Reynold A. Nicholson (London: Cambridge University Press, 1926), 1:97.
[30] Rumi, *Mathnawi*, book 1: 620–29, trans. Reynold A. Nicholson (London: Cambridge University Press, 1926), 1:36.

PART II HUMAN NATURE AND SUFFERING

Pastoral and Spiritual Responses to Sickness

Patience and Trust in God

One of the most important responses to illness is to put your trust in God and respond to sickness with patience. One of the best examples in the tradition is the prophet Job, a biblical figure who is also mentioned in the Qur'an. According to the tradition, Job was inflicted with a severe illness. But despite his suffering, he turned to God with humility and prayer. Job represents the archetype of patience in Islam. The Qur'an alludes to this character as follows: "Indeed We found him to be patient in adversity. What an excellent servant! He always turned to God."[31] In another verse, the Qur'an brings up Job's prayer in the midst of severe suffering: "Remember Job, when he cried out to his Lord, saying: 'Suffering has truly afflicted me, but you are the Most Merciful of the merciful.'"[32]

Physical Illness versus Spiritual Illness

Some Muslim scholars have interpreted Job's complaint as concern about his spirituality, because his physical suffering became so severe that it prevented him from worshipping.[33] That is why these scholars often point to nonphysical illnesses. To them, the major sicknesses that believers should be worried about are the spiritual diseases of the heart. In this context, this tradition of the Prophet Muhammad is frequently quoted: "Beware! There is a piece of flesh in the body, if it remains healthy the whole body becomes healthy, and if it is diseased, the whole body becomes diseased. Beware, it is the heart."[34]

Sin and transgression, relying on something other than God, hypocrisy, falling into despair, heedlessness, hatred, arrogance,

[31] Qur'an 38:44.
[32] Qur'an 21:83.
[33] Nursi, Lem'alar, 32.
[34] Sahih al-Bukhari: kitab al-iman, bab fadl man istabra' li dinih.

120

ILLNESS AND HEALING

envy, negative thoughts about others, being ungrateful, showing off, and love of the world are among the spiritual diseases of the heart. In order to deal with these illnesses, Muslim scholars have focused on the purification of the self (*tazkiyah al-nafs*). This is especially emphasized in Sufism.

Purifying the self (*nafs*) is one of Sufism's most important goals, and "The one who knows his self knows God" has become an important mantra in Sufi spirituality. Sufis regard the self as an even greater enemy than Satan. Dealing with the desires of the self is presented as the greatest jihad.[35] The Qur'an instructs believers that they should not claim their selves to be pure.[36] Al-Ghazali (d. 1111), who is also known for outlining the orthodox views within Sufism, dedicated one of his treatises to fighting the ego (*jihad al-nafs*) in his magnum opus, *Ihya' 'Ulum al-Din*. In this work, al-Ghazali highlights the importance of jihad against the ego:

> Know that the body is like a town and the intellect of the mature human being is like a king ruling that town. Its armies are the external and internal senses and its subject are its organs. The ego that commands evil [*nafs ammara*] which is manifested in desires and anger, is like an enemy that contests him in his kingdom and fights to kill his people. The body thus becomes like a battleground and the soul is its guard. If he fights against his enemies and defeats them and compels them to do what he likes, he will be praised when he returns to God's presence, as God said: "Allah favors those who strive with their wealth and lives a degree above those who stay behind." (Qur'an 4:95)[37]

Here Ghazali indicates that the self should always be armed against the evil commanding ego as if it is at war because it is a threat to the spiritual well-being of a believer. That is why Sufi scholars

---

[35] Carl Ernst, *Sufism: An Introduction to the Mystical Tradition of Islam* (Boston: Shambhala, 2011), 104.

[36] Qur'an 53:32.

[37] Al-Ghazali, *Ihya' 'Ulum al-Din* (Cairo: Al-Quds, 2012), 3:11.

121

PART II HUMAN NATURE AND SUFFERING

offered various guidelines for their disciples to purify their selves in order to overcome the spiritual diseases of the heart. Al-Qushayri (d. 1074), for example, listed fifty spiritual stations for the journey. Among them are repentance (*tawba*), solitariness (*uzla*), abstinence (*wara*), asceticism (*zuhd*), silence (*samt*), hunger (*ju*), abandoning desire (*tark al-shahwa*), humility (*tawadu*), opposition to the soul or ego (*mukhalafat al-nafs*), contentment (*qanaa*), trust in God (*tawakkul*), thankfulness (*shukr*), patience (*sabr*), sincerity (*ikhlas*), remembrance of God (*dhikr*), manners (*adab*), prayer (*dua*), poverty (*faqr*), gnosis (*marifa*), love (*mahabba*), and yearning (*shawq*).[38]

Like al-Qushayri, Imam Muhammad Mawlud (d. 1905), a Mauritanian scholar, also provided treatment for his students:

> A comprehensive treatment plan for the heart's diseases is to deny the self of its desires,
> enjoin hunger, keep worship vigilance in the night, silence and meditation in private;
> also keeping company with good people who possess sincerity, those who are emulated in their states and statements;
> and, finally, taking refuge in the One unto whom all affairs return. That is the most beneficial treatment for all of the previous diseases.
> This must be to the point in which you are like a man drowning or someone lost in a barren desert and sees no source of succor except from the Guardian, possessor of the greatest power. He is the One who responds to the call of the distressed.[39]

Prayer and Worship

The time of sickness is considered an opportunity for prayer and worship. Because while believers should be grateful and thankful

[38] Ernst, *Sufism*, 104.

[39] Imam al-Mawlud, *Purification of the Heart: Signs, Symptoms and Cures of the Spiritual Diseases of the Heart*, trans. Hamza Yusuf (Mountain View, CA: Sandala, 2012), 90.

122

ILLNESS AND HEALING

during prosperous times, they should also turn to God during difficult times, including sickness. It is reported that Muhammad did not give up on his prayers and worship during his severe illnesses. He would still perform the five daily prayers (*salat*). Given that it requires many physical movements, believers can perform their prayers even with the movement of their eyes.

Visiting the Sick

Visiting the sick is among the key responses to sickness that are deeply embedded in Islamic societies. The hadith collections often include a book on this teaching. Muhammad taught his followers that visiting the sick is a major duty of fellow Muslims toward one another.[40] He also reminded them of its merits. The Prophet reported that on the day of the resurrection, God will say:

> O son of Adam, I fell ill and you visited Me not. He will say: O Lord, and how should I visit You when You are the Lord of the worlds? He will say: Did you not know that My servant so and so had fallen ill and you visited him not? Did you not know that had you visited him you would have found Me with him? O son of Adam, I asked you for food and you fed Me not. He will say: O Lord, and how should I feed You when You are the Lord of the worlds? He will say: Did you not know that My servant so and so asked you for food and you fed him not? Did you not know that had you fed him you would surely have found that (the reward for doing so) with Me? O son of Adam, I asked you to give Me to drink and you gave Me not to drink. He will say: O Lord, how should I give You to drink when You are the Lord of the worlds? He will say: My servant So-and-so asked you to give him to drink and you gave him not to drink. Had you given him to drink you would have surely found that with Me.[41]

---

[40] *Sahih al-Bukhari: kitab al-libas, bab al-mithara al-hamra'.*
[41] Al-Bukhari, *al-Adab al-Mufrad: kitab 'iyad al-marda, bab 'iyadah al-marda.*

PART II HUMAN NATURE AND SUFFERING

The implication of this hadith is that there is a divine presence and blessing in taking care of the most vulnerable and needy, including those who are sick. Visiting the sick can be a means of being closer to God, because in another report, Muhammad said: "When Muslims visit a sick person at dawn, seventy thousand angels keep on praying for them till dusk. If they visit the person in the evening, seventy thousand angels keep on praying for them till the morning; and they will have their share of reaped fruits in heaven."[42]

Illness is part of human nature. Muslims turn to God for their physical and spiritual illnesses because God is not only the creator of sickness; he is also the healer. They also seek remedies from the Qur'an, the teachings of Muhammad, the spiritual paths of scholars, and modern medicine. In Chapter 7, I discuss another aspect of life: death and suffering.

---

[42] *Jami' al-Tirmidhi: kitab al-janaiz, bab ma ja'a fi 'iyadah al-marid.*

7 | Death, Resurrection, and the Hereafter

Mahommah Baquaqua was born in 1824 into a noble Muslim family in Djougou, Benin, in West Africa. As a young man, Mahommah was sold to European traders and eventually taken to Brazil. In 1847, he traveled on a ship transporting coffee to New York, from where he was able to escape with the help of abolitionists. On his journey from West Africa to New York, Mahommah had been owned by many different slave masters.[1] Under them, he suffered such brutality that he attempted to drown himself during his captivity in Brazil. Referring to the abuses and cruelties he endured at the hands of one of his masters, Mahommah wrote:

> But the day is coming when his power will be vested in another, and of his stewardship he must render an account; alas what account can he render of the crimes committed upon the writhing bodies of the poor pitiless wretches he had under his charge; when his kingship shall cease and the great accounting be called for; how shall he answer?[2]

In his statement, Mahommah was pointing to the day of judgment. In times of suffering and grief, he found hope in the Islamic theology of the hereafter and the accountability it promises.

---

[1] For more information about Baquaqua, see Mahommah Gardo Baquaqua and Samuel Moore, *Biography of Mahommah G. Baquaqua, a Native of Zoogoo, in the Interior of Africa* [...] (Detroit: Geo. E. Pomeroy, 1854), https://docsouth.unc.edu/neh/baquaqua/summary.html.

[2] Quoted in Kambiz GhaneaBassiri, *A History of Islam in America* (Cambridge: Cambridge University Press, 2010), 91.

PART II HUMAN NATURE AND SUFFERING

Belief in life after death has been part of the creeds of many religions. It is one of the six articles of faith in Islam. Perhaps no religious scripture is concerned with life after death as much as the Qur'an. Descriptions of heaven and hell are quite vivid in Muslim scripture. One can find almost no passage that does not reference the hereafter, and interestingly, belief in God and the hereafter are often juxtaposed in the same verses. The Qur'an presents faith in the hereafter as a common belief of Islam, Christianity, and Judaism.[3]

The Qur'an on the Resurrection of the Body

We know from the Qur'an that the Meccan polytheists did not believe in life after death.[4] They rejected the Prophet's message of resurrection and accountability on the day of judgment, arguing: "There is nothing beyond our first death, and we shall not be resurrected."[5] The Qur'an explains their view as claiming that "there is no life but our worldly life. We die and live, and nothing destroys us except time."[6] The Meccans also challenged the Prophet by calling on him to bring their ancestors back to life.[7] The Qur'an states that they had no knowledge of the hereafter and only followed their own desires. It is God who gives life, causes people to die, and gathers them on the day of resurrection.[8]

In other passages, the disbelievers of Mecca get more specific in their view of the resurrection: "What! When we and our forefathers have become dust, shall we really be raised from the dead? We have heard such promises before, and so did our forefathers. These are nothing but tales of the ancients."[9] In another verse, the Qur'an

[3] Qur'an 3:114.
[4] Qur'an 16:38.
[5] Qur'an 44:35–36.
[6] Qur'an 45:24.
[7] Qur'an 45:25.
[8] Qur'an 45:26.
[9] Qur'an 27:67–68.

126

DEATH, RESURRECTION, AND THE HEREAFTER

relates their accusatory question: "Who can give life to the bones when they are decayed?"[10]

Engaging with the disbelievers' arguments against belief in resurrection and accountability on the day of judgment, the Qur'an provides its own answers. One response is that it is possible for God to resurrect the dead given that he is the Almighty (al-Qadir). To challenge the argument that decayed bones could not be brought to life, the scripture points to the creation of humankind:

Does not man see that We [God] created him from a sperm? Yet behold! He is an open opponent. And he makes comparisons for Us, and forgets his own creation. He says, "Who can give life to the bones when they are decayed?" Say, "He will give them life Who created them for the first time, for He is well-versed in every kind of creation. It is He who made fire for you from the green tree, and behold, you kindle from it." Is not He Who created the heavens and the earth able to create the like of them? Yes, indeed. He is the All Knowing Creator. When He wills something to be, His way is to say, "Be!" and it is! So, glory be to Him in whose Hand lies the dominion of all things. It is to Him that you will be returned.[11]

The Qur'an also alludes to spring as evidence of resurrection: "Look, then, at the imprints of God's mercy, how He gives life to the earth after its death. This same God is the one who will give life to the dead. He has power over all things."[12] In another place, it points to signs of resurrection in the creation: "And how We send blessed water down from the sky and grow with it gardens, the harvested grain, and the lofty date palms with ranged clusters, as a provision for God's servants; and We give new life with it to land that is dead."[13] The passage concludes that similarly, "this is how the resurrection of

[10] Qur'an 36:78.
[11] Qur'an 36:77–83.
[12] Qur'an 30:50.
[13] Qur'an 50:9–11.

127

PART II HUMAN NATURE AND SUFFERING

the dead will be."[14] The Qur'an also indicates that resurrection is as easy as the creation of one being: "Your creation and your resurrection are only as the creation and resurrection of a single soul."[15]

Theology of the Hereafter

Muslim theologians approach the subject of the hereafter through God's attributes, because the manifestations of God's names require both resurrection and human accountability. God is the One Who Creates with Wisdom and Purpose (al-Hakim); therefore, nothing is created in vain. God creates humans who reflect his own attributes. If human lives concluded with death alone, this would contradict his wisdom, and human life as such would be a waste. Why would the most precious and most intelligent creature of creation die to no avail? Moreover, humans desire eternity; they long to live forever. God has equipped human nature with this desire. If God is loving and compassionate toward creation, why would he not fulfill the human desire for eternity? Similarly, one of God's names is the Just One (al-'Adl), which refers to the divine notion of harmony, order, and balance in both this world and the next. While humans long for justice and are encouraged to strive toward it, there remains much injustice in this world. Those who commit major crimes against their fellow humans often get away with their misdeeds. Many leave this world without ever being held fully accountable. There are people who are born into suffering. People often face injustice despite being good natured and innocent. Is this consistent with God's justice?

A case in point is the tragic story of Christine Jessop, a nine-year-old girl who went missing on October 3, 1984, in Ontario, Canada. Her body was found three months later. Christine had been raped and murdered. Guy Paul Morin, Jessop's neighbor, was

---

[14] Qur'an 50:9–11.
[15] Qur'an 31:28.

128

DEATH, RESURRECTION, AND THE HEREAFTER

charged with her death. However, Morin was exonerated in 1995 after serving eighteen months in prison. Police were able to identify the killer, Calvin Hoover, in 2020 by using a new investigative technique called genetic genealogy. What made this incident even more complicated is that Hoover had committed suicide in 2015.[16] This is just one example of unresolved justice. Hoover left this world with dignity, and he is not the only one. There are so many people, including Adolf Hitler and Saddam Hussein, who leave this world without being held accountable for their enormous crimes. The justice in this world remains insufficient to comfort and compensate their innocent victims. Human accountability on the day of judgment will rectify those injustices and bring balance and order to God's creation. Those who have promoted goodness in this world will eventually be rewarded, and those who have caused evil and suffering will be held accountable and face their rightful punishment – unless they have sought forgiveness and repentance.

Considering that injustice often happens in secret, the Qur'an repeatedly emphasizes that God sees everything and that there is nothing that is outside of his knowledge: "He knows what is in the heavens and the earth; He knows what you hide and what you disclose; God knows well the secrets of all hearts."[17] In one of the hadiths, the Prophet said: "On the day of judgment a sheep without horn will take its right from a sheep with horn."[18] The Qur'an highlights that even if people get away with their injustices here on earth, they will eventually have to face the ultimate judge who awaits them in the hereafter. Since the divine attributes are reflected in this world only in a dim and limited manner, God's name the Just One (al-'Adl), along with many of his other qualities, will be fully revealed in the afterlife.

---

[16] Ronna Syed and Shanifa Nasser, "Toronto Police Identify Killer in Cold Case of 9 Year Old Christine Jessop," *CBC*, October 15, 2020, www.cbc.ca/news/canada/toronto/christine-jessop-news-conference-1.5763673.

[17] Qur'an 64:4.

[18] *Jami' al-Tirmidhi: kitab al-qiyamah, bab ma ja'a fi sha'n al-hisab wa al-qisas.*

PART II HUMAN NATURE AND SUFFERING

Death as a Creation of God

According to Islamic eschatology, this world will end (*qiyama*), leading to the hereafter. God will resurrect everyone from the dead and gather them on the day of judgment. Human beings will then be held accountable for their actions – good or bad. For each individual, however, the end of this world begins with one's own death. Remembering death in this world is an important way of being mindful of the hereafter and planning accordingly. The Qur'an repeatedly reminds people of their ultimate destiny – namely, death: "Every soul shall taste death. We test you with evil and with good, and to Us you will be returned."[19] In another verse, the Qur'an points out that "death will overtake you no matter where you may be, even inside high towers."[20] Nevertheless, death is seen as a sign of God's creation or the manifestation of his name the Bringer of Death (al-Mumit). It is also part of God's design.

Like life, God creates death. It comes as no surprise, then, that Islamic theology often depicts death positively. It is not a departure but rather a step forward to a new beginning. Whenever Muslims hear of the death of a loved one, they invoke the Qur'anic phrase: "We belong to God and to Him we shall return."[21] The poet Rumi (d. 1273) wrote about his future death and funeral in a way that eloquently captures the Islamic approach to death:

> On the day of (my) death when my coffin is going (by),
> Don't imagine that I have (any) pain (about leaving) this world.

> Don't weep for me, and don't say, "How terrible! What a pity!"
> (For) you will fall into the error of (being deceived by) the
>   Devil, (and) that would (really) be a pity!

> When you see my funeral, don't say, "Parting and separation!"
> (Since) for me, that is the time for union and meeting (God).

[19] Qur'an 21:35.
[20] Qur'an 4:78.
[21] Qur'an 2:156.

DEATH, RESURRECTION, AND THE HEREAFTER

(And when) you entrust me to the grave, don't say,
"Good-bye! Farewell!" For the grave is (only) a curtain for
(hiding) the gathering (of souls) in Paradise.

When you see the going down, notice the coming up. Why should
there be (any) loss because of the setting of the sun and moon?

It seems like setting to you, but it is rising. The tomb seems like a
prison, (but) it is the liberation of the soul.

What seed (ever) went down into the earth which didn't grow
(back up)? (So), for you, why is there this doubt about the human
"seed"?

What bucket (ever) went down and didn't come out full? Why
should there be (any) lamenting for the Joseph of the soul because
of the well?

When you have closed (your) mouth on this side, open (it) on
that side, for your shouts of joy will be in the Sky beyond place
(and time).[22]

God would not have taken the Prophet Muhammad's life if death
were not beautiful, as another poet put it.[23] While it appears that a
seed dies and disintegrates, in reality, it yields life. Likewise, the death
of humans should be regarded not as destruction or an end but rather
as "the sign, introduction, and starting point of perpetual life."[24]

Muslims still mourn death but do so with the conviction that
death is not an end; it is a new beginning. The Prophet's own experience reflects this philosophy. He had seven children, and six of
them died before him. When the Prophet's son Ibrahim died in
infancy, his companions saw him weeping. They asked him: "Do
you mourn the dead too?" The Prophet answered that in the face of

---

[22] Jalaluddin Rumi, "On the Day of My Death," in *Diwan-e Kabir*, trans. Ibrahim Gamard, available at Dar-Al-Masnavi, accessed May 17, 2020, www.dar-al-masnavi.org/gh-0911.html.

[23] Necip Fazıl Kisakürek, *Çile* (Istanbul: Büyük Doğu Yayınları, 2014), 298.

[24] Nursi, *Letters*, 284.

PART II HUMAN NATURE AND SUFFERING

the death of our loved ones, "the eyes will weep; the heart gets sad. However, we will invoke the words that are pleasing to our Lord." The Prophet then turned to his dead son: "If there was no hope in death, and if it were not the destiny of everyone, and if those were left behind would not be united with those who die, we would be in even more grief. We exceedingly mourn your death."[25]

Suicide and Euthanasia

Because the body is considered sacred, suicide is forbidden in Islamic jurisprudence. This approach is based on some of the teachings of the Qur'an and Muhammad. The Muslim scripture, for example, says: "Do not take life, which God has made sacred, except by a just cause."[26] It also mentions that killing an innocent person is like killing all of humanity, and saving the life of an innocent person is like saving the lives of all people.[27] God is the one who gives and takes life. The time of death is assigned by him. In this regard, the Qur'an reads: "When their time arrives, they cannot delay it for a moment, nor can they advance it."[28] In another verse, the Qur'an reminds us that "no one can die except with God's permission at a predestined time."[29] The impermissibility of suicide is reported in a number of hadiths as well. In one of them, Muhammad said: "Amongst the nations before you there was a man who got a wound. Growing impatient with its pain, he took a knife and cut his hand with which led to his death. God then said, 'My servant hurried to bring death upon himself so I have forbidden him to enter Paradise.'"[30] In another tradition, the Prophet stated: "None of you should desire

[25] *Hadislerle Islam* (Istanbul: Diyanet İşleri Başkanlığı, 2014), 7:549.
[26] Qur'an 17:33.
[27] Qur'an 5:32.
[28] Qur'an 16:61.
[29] Qur'an 3:145.
[30] *Sahih al-Bukhari: kitab ahadi al-anbiya, bab ma dhukira 'an bani israil.*

DEATH, RESURRECTION, AND THE HEREAFTER

death because your pain and suffering. Instead you should pray as follows: O God if living is better for me then keep me alive, if death is better for me then take my life."[31] Based on the same premises, the overwhelming majority of Muslim scholars have concluded that "active" euthanasia and physician-assisted suicide are also forbidden in Islam. However, many of them believe that "passive" euthanasia is considered permissible in certain conditions. In the case of terminally ill patients, for example, if death is inevitable because of brain death or the patient is in a permanent vegetative state, then the life support can be turned off.[32] Taking one's life because of major psychological problems or losing sanity and consciousness is not discussed in the context of suicide. The tradition considers suicide as a major sin only if it is committed by a sane and conscious person.[33]

Contemplating Death and the Hereafter

Contemplating death and the hereafter is an essential aspect of Islamic spirituality. A companion of the Prophet was asked about a common supplication that the messenger would address to God. He answered that Muhammad would pray: "Oh God, give us goodness in this world and the hereafter and protect us from the hellfire."[34] The Qur'an relates that one of the prayers of Abraham was: "Our Lord, forgive me, my parents, and the believers on the Day when the Reckoning shall take place."[35] Moses prayed in this manner: "And ordain for us good in this world and in the Hereafter. We turn repentant to You."[36]

---

[31] Sahih al-Bukhari: kitab al-marda, bab tamanni al-marid al-mawt.

[32] Rishad Raffi Motlani, "Islam, Euthanasia and Western Christianity: Drawing on Western Christian Thinking to Develop an Expanded Western Sunni Muslim Perspective on Euthanasia" (PhD diss., University of Exeter, 2011), 220–21.

[33] Hadislerle Islam (Istanbul: Diyanet İşleri Başkanlığı, 2014), 5:510.

[34] Sahih Muslim: kitab al-dhikr wa al-du'a' wa al-tawbah wa al-istighfar, bab fadl majalis al-dhikr.

[35] Qur'an 14:41.

[36] Qur'an 7:156.

PART II HUMAN NATURE AND SUFFERING

Islamic spirituality aims to maintain a balance between this world and the hereafter. The Prophet said: "For a believer the highest concern is the concern for both this world and the hereafter."[37] While Islam does not encourage an ascetic or monastic life by which believers will retreat from eating, drinking, sleeping, and marriage, it discourages them from being overly attached to this world. In other words, the work of this world should not come at the expense of one's relationship with God or their work for the hereafter. The Qur'an explains:

> Men whom neither merchandise nor sale can divert from the remembrance of God, nor from regular prayer, nor from the practice of regular charity: Their only fear is for the Day when hearts and eyes will be overturned. That God may reward them according to the best of their deeds and add even more for them out of His grace, for God provides for whomever he pleases without measure.[38]

That is why the following statement has become a mantra among Muslims: Work for this world as if you will never die, and work for the hereafter as if you will die tomorrow.

Even today, whenever individual or communal prayer takes place among Muslims, the hereafter is remembered. Invoking death is regarded as being mindful of God and the impermanence of the world. Once people internalize the idea that everything but God is subject to departure and death, they will refrain from attaching their hearts to ephemeral things.

Death is also mentioned in the story of Joseph, which the Qur'an calls "the best of stories."[39] At the end of the narrative, Joseph asks God to make him die in righteousness.[40] When a happy story ends with a reminder of death and separation, it generally diminishes the reader's joy and makes the story more painful for them. But in the

---

[37] Muhammad b. Yazid Ibn Majah, *Sunan Ibn Majah: kitab al-tijarat, bab al-iqtisad fi talab al-ma'ishah.*

[38] Qur'an 24:37–38.

[39] Qur'an 12:3.

[40] Qur'an 12:101.

134

DEATH, RESURRECTION, AND THE HEREAFTER

Qur'anic account, death is mentioned when Joseph is at the peak of happiness and joy. Having been betrayed by his brothers and sold into slavery, he has risen to an important rank and, in the end, is reunited with his family. The fact that Joseph remembers death demonstrates his belief that there is greater happiness beyond this worldly life. The end of the story causes readers no sorrow; rather, it gives them hope and enjoyment. Constantly remembering death prevents people from being heedless of God's glory and too attached to the things of this world.[41]

The story of the prophet Abraham in the Qur'an can be read in a similar fashion. In the story, Abraham is searching for his Lord.[42] When night falls, Abraham sees a star and says: "This is my Lord." But when the star sets, he says: "I do not love things that set." Abraham then sees the moon and says: "This is my Lord." But when it too disappears, he realizes it also cannot be his Lord. Upon seeing the sunrise and sunset, he reasons the same way. Abraham's search results in this conclusion: "I turn my face toward Him who created the heavens and the earth. I am not one of the polytheists."[43] The gist of the story is that the heart cannot be attached to those things that are subject to death and departure. When people are attached to such things, they cannot help but be disappointed. Loving things that are subject to death is not worthwhile because those things are not, in reality, beautiful. The heart is created to be the mirror of the love of God; to love things that are eternal precludes the love of ephemeral things.[44]

Death and the Formation of a Virtuous Character

Although it has become less common in modern times, building a virtuous character through the remembrance of death has long

---

[41] Nursi, *Letters*, 335.
[42] For the related story, see Qur'an 6:74–79.
[43] Qur'an 6:79.
[44] Nursi, *Words*, 228.

PART II HUMAN NATURE AND SUFFERING

been a part of religious traditions. For example, the Latin phrase "memento mori" (remember that you must die) was a mantra in medieval Christianity – an important practice in building good character. Such practices have been equally important in the Islamic tradition. The hadith collections usually include a book of *janaiz* (funerals), which is devoted to the subject of death. The Sufi tradition also takes the remembrance of death as a significant element of its spirituality and the formation of a virtuous character. The last – and longest – book of al-Ghazali's *Ihya' al-'Ulum ad-Din* is dedicated to death and the hereafter.

Muslims consider remembering death to be a means of forming a virtuous character. It can be an important way to attain sincerity. Pretentiousness and excessive attachment to possessions are obstacles to sincerity. The reality of death keeps believers from pretentiousness and protects them from the traps of their own egos. This is why Muslims often recite Qur'anic verses such as "Every soul shall taste death" and "Truly you will die one day, and truly they too will die one day," as contemplating that death is a significant part of their spiritual lives.[45] Constantly thinking of one's own death brings the faithful to an ideal state of sincerity. It leads to a joyful life – one without remorse or regret in the end. Instead, pondering one's death leads the believer to appreciate life and live it to the fullest.

The remembrance of death not only fosters self-contemplation and gratitude but makes people humbler and more sensitive toward their fellow humans. When people contemplate the ephemera of this world and think about their mortality, they can be more thoughtful toward one another. In his *Denial of Death*, cultural anthropologist Ernest Becker points out a direct correlation between refusing to face our mortality and fostering conflict. He asserts that when humans face their mortality, the world becomes a better place.[46] As Becker says: "Man's natural and

---

[45] Qur'an 3:185; 39:30. See also Nursi, *Flashes*, 217.
[46] See Ernest Becker, *The Denial of Death* (New York: Free Press, 1997).

DEATH, RESURRECTION, AND THE HEREAFTER

inevitable urge to deny mortality and achieve a heroic self-image are the root causes of human evil."[47]

Contemplating death might also be an important cure for the often destructive emotions of enmity and jealousy. A person whose heart is full of enmity and jealousy toward a rival because of the worldly skills and blessings that rival has should realize that the beauty, strength, rank, and wealth their rival possesses not only are transient and temporary but also might be burdensome.[48]

Death Rituals

Like adherents of other religions, Muslims practice specific death rituals. In the last moments of their lives, Muslims invoke the testimony of faith (*shahadah*). Those around the deathbed should encourage the individual to say: "There is no God but God, and Muhammad is His messenger." In the presence of the dying person, Muslims usually recite the Qur'an, especially chapter 36, "Surat al-Yasin." Before burial, close relatives (ideally) wash the dead body, wrap it in a simple white shroud, and then say a prayer. Based on a prophetic hadith advising Muslims to hasten the funeral rites, it has become an important tradition in Islam to do the washing and the burial as soon as possible.[49]

Attending a funeral service is a communal obligation. However, if enough members in the Muslim community fulfill the obligation, Islamic law allows the remaining Muslims to not attend. In one of the hadiths, the Prophet lists funeral attendance as a fundamental responsibility believers owe to one another.[50]

---

[47] Ernest Becker, *Escape from Evil* (New York: Free Press, 1985), xvii.

[48] Nursi, *Letters*, 315.

[49] *Sahih Muslim: kitab al-jana'iz, bab al-'Isra' bi al-jana'iz.*

[50] *Sahih al-Bukhari: kitab al-jana'iz, bab al-'amr bittiba' al-jana'iz.*

PART II HUMAN NATURE AND SUFFERING

The funeral prayer usually includes a recitation from the Qur'an, especially the first chapter, "Al-Fatiha," and a proclamation of "God is great," as well as other supplications for the deceased and the congregation. Then the one leading the prayers asks the congregation to forgive the dead person for any wrongdoing, after which the congregation proceeds to the graveyard, often with people carrying the coffin together on their shoulders. In the grave, the head is laid in the direction of the Kaaba. Then the mourners close the grave with soil. In the cemetery, the congregation is involved not only in digging the grave but also in helping move the body into the grave. As in Orthodox Judaism, cremation is impermissible in Islam due to the sacredness of the body.

The common belief among Muslims is that physical death marks the separation of the rational soul (*nafs*) and the life-infusing soul or spirit (*ruh*). While the former perishes, the latter continues until the day of resurrection.[51] After burial, the angels of *munkar* and *nakir* will visit the dead person to ask questions about God and the Prophet. According to the tradition, the soul of the deceased will remain in the intermediate realm (*barzakh*) until resurrection on the day of judgment.[52] One's condition in *barzakh* depends on their state of faith and good deeds at the time of death – it can be either a heavenly or hellish waiting room.[53]

The community usually shows support to mourners by offering condolences (*ta'ziya*). Part of the Sunna of the Prophet is also to offer food to the family of the deceased.[54]

Death is a major theme of the Qur'an. It is a creation of God as well as a sign of his power. Despite the suffering that is associated with death, it is seen not as the destruction of a life but rather as a

---

[51] Jane Idleman Smith and Yvonne Yazbeck Haddad, *The Islamic Understanding of Death and Resurrection* (Oxford: Oxford University Press, 2002), 20.

[52] Qur'an 23:99–100.

[53] *Jami' al-Tirmidhi: kitab sifat al-qiyama.*

[54] Mustafa Çağrıcı, "Taziye," in *İslam Ansiklopedisi* (Ankara: TDK, 2011), 40:203.

DEATH, RESURRECTION, AND THE HEREAFTER

transition to the eternal life as well as union with God. Remembering death is a means of building a virtuous character and being mindful of God.

Part III explores three contemporary cases in relation to God, evil, and suffering. I begin with disability followed by the environmental crisis and the coronavirus disease.

Part III | Contemporary Questions

8 | Disability, the Blind, and God's Justice

Sara Minkara is an American Muslim. On her seventh birthday, she woke up and realized that she could not see. Sara's sister had also lost her sight a few years before. Sara's parents assured her that everything would be fine. They were not discouraged by the stigma of blindness in society and did everything in their power to make sure that her disability was not an obstacle. Sara also had a safety net of support provided by the government and private institutions. She went to Wellesley College for her undergraduate studies and received a graduate degree from Harvard University. Sara is also the founder of Empowerment Through Integration, a nonprofit organization dedicated to empowering youth with disabilities around the world. Because of her work and advocacy for people with disabilities, in 2021, President Joe Biden appointed Minkara as the US special advisor on international disability rights.[1]

Sara is an observant Muslim who wears a headscarf. It is not uncommon for her to make references to elements of Islamic theology when she relates to her life story. While she often points to the barriers in Muslim communities against people with disabilities, she also finds strength in her faith. Sara refers to her blindness as the "biggest blessing" of her life.[2] Her parents believed that

---

[1] "President Biden Announces Sara Minkara as United States Special Advisor on International Disability Rights," White House, October 28, 2021, www.whitehouse .gov/briefing-room/statements-releases/2021/10/28/president-biden-announces-sara-minkara-as-united-states-special-advisor-on-international-disability-rights/.

[2] "Enabled by Faith: Sara Minkara," Yaqeen Institute, January 11, 2019, https:// yaqeeninstitute.org/yaqeen-institute/enabled-by-faith-sara-minkara-confident-muslim.

PART III CONTEMPORARY QUESTIONS

her disability was part of God's plan, and what comes from God is a blessing. Instead of asking "Oh God, why us, my daughters?" they believed there was a divine purpose for the disabilities of their daughters. The parents also never allowed the stigma about disability in society to enter their home. They embraced the disability and taught their daughters to do so as well. Blindness became a source of empowerment for the Minkara family. Sara points out that God will never test believers with something that they cannot handle. God is the creator, and he is the one who created her in this way. God only creates what is beautiful, and people with disabilities have something beautiful to contribute to society. Sara also criticizes the negative assumptions about people with disabilities in Muslim societies, as they are often marginalized, pitied, and seen as charity cases.

Sara is not alone in her disability. According to the most recent studies, around a billion people (15 percent of the world's population) experience some form of disability in their lives.[3] The number is increasing significantly.[4] Sixty-one million adults in the United States have some type of disability.[5] That is why those without a disability are frequently called "temporarily abled bodies" in disability studies, since most disabilities are acquired after birth. Disability is often defined as a physical, mental, cognitive, or developmental condition that limits a person's movements, senses, activities, and interactions. However, it is important to recognize the limits of definitions because of the diversity of disabilities.

While there are many models of disability, two of them became more prevalent. One of them is the medical model. According to this model, disability is a medical and individual problem.

[3] "Disability Inclusion," World Bank, accessed January 12, 2022, www.worldbank.org/en/topic/disability#1.

[4] "Disability and Health," World Health Organization, November 24, 2021, www.who.int/news-room/fact-sheets/detail/disability-and-health.

[5] "Disability Impacts All of Us," Centers for Disease Control and Prevention, accessed January 14, 2022, www.cdc.gov/ncbddd/disabilityandhealth/infographic-disability-impacts-all.html.

DISABILITY, THE BLIND, AND GOD'S JUSTICE

The impairment of a person needs to be treated and eliminated because it is a medical condition. The other approach is the social model, which focuses on the barriers that people with disabilities face in society. In this model, people with disabilities are not limited because of their impairments; the impediments are constructed by society. While the model does not disregard the challenges of impairment and its impact on individuals, it also does not view people with disabilities as "objects" of charitable work and social protection. They are "subjects" with equal rights, "capable of claiming those rights, able to make decisions for their own lives based on their free and informed consent and be active members of society."[6]

People have raised questions about and attempted to determine the origins of disability for centuries. The Greek and Roman cultures were concerned with the perfection of the body because beauty and strength mattered in their societies. While a healthy body was seen as a divine blessing, deformity was viewed as a sign of divine wrath. A child with a disability was believed to be an affliction upon the parents from God. Blindness, for example, was interpreted as a divine punishment for sin.[7] Plato believed that children with defects should be abandoned in "mysterious unknown places."[8] The Romans viewed birth defects as an indication of a broken covenant with their gods; so-called monstrous births could incur the wrath of deities.[9] While there have been diverse interpretations of disability in Hinduism and Buddhism, it is usually

[6] "Social Model of Disability," People with Disability Australia, accessed January 25, 2022, https://pwd.org.au/resources/disability-info/social-model-of-disability/.

[7] Susan Baglieri and Arthur Shapiro, *Disability Studies and the Inclusive Classroom: Critical Practices for Creating Least Restrictive Attitudes* (London: Routledge, 2012), 56–57.

[8] Chomba Wa Munyi, "Past and Present Perceptions towards Disability: A Historical Perspective," *Disability Studies Quarterly* 32 (2012): 2, https://dsq-sds .org/article/view/3197/3068&sa=U&ved=0ahUKEwjIpcnIlubKAhULaz4KHX_ YDyoQFggoMAc&usg=AFQjCNEWDZ_ojsTkoB8Q2JDebeZ2Ngp2QQ.

[9] Vardit Rispler-Chaim, *Disability in Islamic Law* (Dordrecht: Springer, 2007), 5.

145

PART III CONTEMPORARY QUESTIONS

associated with the concept of karma in these dharmic traditions. Disability might be related to a person's actions in the past or their parents' actions.[10] In Judaism, disability is seen as part of God's creation. Examples of God punishing people because of their disobedience are part of the narratives of the Hebrew Bible, where breaking the covenant may result in certain disabilities, including blindness and madness.[11] In the New Testament, we repeatedly see Jesus healing people with disabilities miraculously. There are many examples in which Jesus cares and shows compassion for people with disabilities. However, it is not uncommon for disability to be seen as caused by sin and its healing as a means of purification and grace in Christian theology.[12]

Islamic tradition also addresses the question of disability. In what follows, we explore people with disabilities in the sacred sources of Islam as well as its theology. We begin with the Qur'an.

The Qur'an and People with Disabilities

While there is no one term that refers to disability in the Qur'an, there are a number of occasions where it engages with people with disabilities. The Qur'an's attitude toward disability is most evident in a story that is mentioned in chapter 80. One day, Abdullah bin Umm Maktum, a blind man, came to Muhammad seeking his guidance. At the time, the Prophet was in conversation with a number

---

[10] Arie Rimmerman, *Disability and Community Living Policies* (Cambridge: Cambridge University Press, 2017), 15–16; Susan L. Gabel and Jagdish Chander, "Inclusion in Indian Education," in *Disability and Politics of Education: An International Reader*, ed. Susan L. Gabel and Scot Danforth (New York: Peter Lang, 2008), 72–73.

[11] Deut. 28:28–29.

[12] Pauline A. Otieno, "Biblical and Theological Perspectives on Disability: Implications on the Rights of Persons with Disability in Kenya," *Disability Studies Quarterly* 29 (2009): 4, https://dsq-sds.org/article/view/988/1164.

DISABILITY, THE BLIND, AND GOD'S JUSTICE

of elites of Meccan society conveying the message of Islam. When Abdullah kept asking for guidance, the Prophet then frowned at him and continued his conversation with the unbelievers. Upon this case, the first ten verses in the chapter were revealed, in which God admonished Muhammad for frowning at the blind man. The same chapter of the Qur'an also takes its name from the occasion, "He Frowned" ("Abasa").[13] This became an occasion of learning for the Prophet and his followers. The Qur'an was delivering a clear message: Those who are blind to the truth in their hearts should not be preferred to a blind person who is open to and seeking the truth. Also, it is likely that the Prophet thought if he could convince the Meccan elite to become Muslim, their contribution to the Muslim community would be greater than the work of an old disabled person. The Qur'an challenges this approach, as people's contributions and spiritual growth cannot be judged according to their rank and appearance.

Ibn Umm Maktum was at the center of another occasion of revelation. When it was revealed that those who attend the war to defend the Muslim community and those who stay at home are not equal, Ibn Umm Maktum told the Prophet that he is unable to attend because of his blindness. Another verse was then revealed, excusing the disabled from participating in wars. Ibn Umm Maktum still participated in a war with a major role and died on the battlefield.

It is reported that whenever Muhammad would see Ibn Umm Maktum, he would greet him by saying: "Welcome to him on whose account my Lord rebuked me."[14] Ibn Umm Maktum remained a key companion of the Prophet. He was sent to Medina as a teacher alongside Musab ibn Umayr prior to the Prophet's immigration.[15]

---

[13] Joseph E. B. Lumbard, "Commentary on *Surat 'Abasa*," in Nasr et al., *Study Quran*, 1475.

[14] Lumbard, 1474.

[15] *Sahih al-Bukhari: kitab manaqib al-ansar, bab maqdam al-nabiy sal al-allah 'alayh wa salam wa ashab al-madinah.*

PART III CONTEMPORARY QUESTIONS

During the Prophet's time in Medina, Ibn Umm Maktum served as the person who issues the call to prayer (*muezzin*) for the Prophet's mosque (Masjid al-Nabawi). Also, if the Prophet left Medina, he would put Ibn Umm Maktum in charge of the city.[16] He would even lead the prayer.

Another major example of disability is the story of Moses. The Qur'an mentions that Moses had a speech impediment, and Pharaoh belittled him because of his impairment: "Am I not better than this fellow, who is despicable and can hardly express himself clearly?"[17] Moses prayed for God to untie the knot from his tongue.[18] God eventually removed his impediment, and Moses was able to convey his message to Pharaoh and his people.[19] The Qur'an also relates the story of the prophet Jacob, who lost his sight because of his sadness concerning the disappearance of his son Joseph. His sight was eventually restored when he was gifted with Joseph's shirt and placed it on his eyes.[20] Like the New Testament, the Qur'an brings up how Jesus healed the disabled. With God's permission, Jesus would cure the blind and the leper and give life to the dead.[21]

The Qur'an also uses disability as a metaphor to convey its message. For example, verse 58 in chapter 40 reads: "The blind and the seeing are not equal, nor are those who believe and perform righteous deeds and the evildoer. How seldom do you keep this in mind!"[22] In another place, the Qur'an uses a different analogy: "The worst creatures in the sight of God are the deaf and the dumb who do not use their reason. If God had known there was any good in them, He would have made them hear, but

[16] *Hadislerle Islam* (Istanbul: Diyanet İşleri Başkanlığı, 2014), 4:268.
[17] Qur'an 43:52.
[18] Qur'an 20:27.
[19] Qur'an 20:36.
[20] Qur'an 12:96.
[21] Qur'an 3:49.
[22] Also see Qur'an 35:19–20.

DISABILITY, THE BLIND, AND GOD'S JUSTICE

even if He had, they would still have turned away in rejection."[23] Muslim scholars do not interpret these verses literally. With these passages, the spiritual disability of humans is emphasized. In the Qur'anic picture of community, people with disabilities are active participants, and they are a key dimension of forming a collective identity.[24] One can observe a similar approach in the life of Muhammad and his relationship with people with disabilities as well.

Muhammad and People with Disabilities

Muhammad had a number of disabled companions who were active participants in the Muslim community. One of them was Muaz Ibn Jabal, who served as the governor of Yemen. It is reported that one of the blind companions came to Muhammad and complained that it was difficult for him to go to the closest mosque in his neighborhood because of his disability. He asked the Prophet to come to his house and pray with him. Muhammad accepted his invitation and went to the companion's house and prayed and enjoyed a meal with him.[25] In another case, Abu Bakr, a close companion of the Prophet, and his father came to the mosque to see the Prophet right after the conquest of Mecca. Abu Bakr's father had lost his sight in old age. When the Prophet saw the old man, he turned to Abu Bakr and said: "Why did you not leave the old man in his house so that I could come to him there?"[26]

In one of the hadiths, it is reported that Muhammad said that God looks not at one's appearance and property but at their heart

---

[23] Qur'an 8:22–23.

[24] Staffan Bengtsson, "Building a Community: Disability and Identity in the Qur'an," *Scandinavian Journal of Disability Research* 20 (2018): 1, www.sjdr.se/articles/10.16993/sjdr.18/.

[25] *Sahih al-Bukhari: kitab al-tahajjud bab salat al-nawafil jama'ah.*

[26] *Hadislerle Islam*, 4:269.

PART III CONTEMPORARY QUESTIONS

and deeds.[27] The point is that no one will be judged based on the way they look or what disabilities they might have. What matters is whether they have a pure heart and good actions.

Islamic Law and Disability

Muhammad's and the Qur'an's approaches to disability are also manifested in Islamic law. Muslim scholars took this Qur'anic teaching as their departure point: "God does not burden any soul beyond its capacity."[28] Experts of jurisprudence made certain accommodations for the participation of physically disabled people in religious practices.[29] They advanced the situation of people with disabilities based on the Prophet's care and compassion in their writings.[30] In any discussions about the practices of Islam, people with disabilities were included, and their obligations were discussed like any other Muslim.[31]

The books of jurisprudence discuss the questions of people with disabilities in the context of worship and rituals (*ibadat*) such as the five daily prayers, fasting, pilgrimage, transactions (*muamalat*), marriage and divorce, crimes (*hudud*), and leadership. Classical Islamic texts of law address the issues concerning disability along with people without a disability. Disability was not discussed in the books of law in a separate section. For example, in the case of blind people, the schools of jurisprudence examined whether they could lead the prayer (be an imam). The overwhelming majority

---

[27] *Sahih Muslim: kitab al-birr wa al-salah wa al-adab, bab tahrim al-zulm al-muslim wa al-khadhlih wahtiqarih wa damihi wa 'irdihi wa malihi.*

[28] Qur'an 2:286.

[29] Kristina L. Richardson, *Difference and Disability in the Medieval Islamic World: Blighted Bodies* (Edinburgh: Edinburgh University Press, 2014), 22.

[30] Ali Altaf Mian, "Mental Disability in Medieval Hanafi Legalism," *Islamic Studies* 51:3 (2012): 262.

[31] Mohammed Ghaly, "Disability in the Islamic Tradition," *Religion Compass* 10:6 (2016): 155.

DISABILITY, THE BLIND, AND GOD'S JUSTICE

of scholars maintained that it is permissible for a blind person to guide the ritual. For the permissibility, they pointed to the reports about the companions who led the prayer during the Prophet's time. Also, having sight is not one of the requirements of leading the prayer. However, scholars still argued that a nonblind person is preferable to a blind person when it comes to conducting the prayer. The cleanliness of clothes and the space for the prayer are important. Also, the imam should know the time of the prayer as well as the direction to the Kaaba. The scholars' concern was that a blind person may be in need of help for these requirements. To fulfill these conditions, it is safer to have a nonblind person lead the prayer. However, there are a number of scholars who argued that a nonblind person should not be preferred to a blind person. There are advantages on both sides. For example, a blind imam would be less distracted by their surroundings, and they can concentrate on the prayer better. Unlike a blind person, a sighted person can pay more attention to the cleanliness of dress and space for the prayer.[32]

While Muslim jurists attempted to further the Qur'anic and the prophetic care and compassion for people with disabilities, it does not mean that their rulings were always practiced in Muslim societies. A case in point is a major mosque that was officially opened in the state of Maryland in the United States in 2016. It was constructed to replicate Ottoman architecture. A prominent element inside the mosque is a pulpit (*minbar*). This is where the leader of the congregation stands to deliver a sermon during Friday or holiday (*eid*) prayer. Like in other major Ottoman mosques, the pulpit has a nine-step staircase. The regulations of the state of Maryland require access to the pulpit for people with disabilities, and as such the pulpit needed either a ramp or an elevator. In order to deal with this complication, the representative of the mosque told state officials that a disabled person is ineligible to give a sermon and lead

---

[32] Hilal Özay, "İslam Hukukunda Bedensel Hükümlere Tesiri Bakımından Bedensel Engel" (PhD diss., Selçuk Üniversitesi, 2010), 126–28.

PART III CONTEMPORARY QUESTIONS

the prayer according to Islamic tradition.[33] He wanted to preserve the traditional architectural form of the pulpit. For him, installing a ramp or an elevator would distort the aesthetic of the pulpit. In this situation, appearance is preferred to accessibility. It excludes people with disabilities. Unfortunately, mosques are often known for their inaccessibility. In order to address this problem, a number of Muslims in the United States founded an organization called Muhsen in 2014. Among Muhsen's services is a three-tiered certificate program (silver, gold, and platinum) for mosques in order to make them more accommodating for Muslims with special needs. Currently, there are around 3,000 mosques in the United States. So far, only seventy-five of them had received the certification, and among those, only a handful have qualified for the gold certificate, while none are eligible for the platinum.[34]

Theological Views on Disability

Disability is an important theme of Islamic theology as well. There are a number of principles from the Qur'an that can be departure points for the theological discussions concerning disability and the problem of evil and suffering. First, misfortunes can only happen with God's permission.[35] Second, God is not only compassionate and merciful; he is also just.[36] Third, God created humans in the best form.[37] Whatever God creates, he creates beautifully.[38] God is also the one who creates human faculties:

[33] Yaşar Çolak, *Din, Siyaset ve Mimari: Amerika Diyanet Merkezinin Tarihi* (Istanbul: Kopernik, 2021), 71.

[34] For the organization and the list of the mosques that received the certificate, see "MUHSEN Masjid Certification," MUHSEN, accessed March 23, 2022, https:// muhsen.org/muhsen-masjid-certification/.

[35] Qur'an 64:11.

[36] Qur'an 4:40.

[37] Qur'an 95:4.

[38] Qur'an 32:7.

DISABILITY, THE BLIND, AND GOD'S JUSTICE

Then He fashioned him, and breathed into him of His Spirit. He gave you hearing, sight, and hearts. How little do you give thanks![39]

Have We not given them two eyes, a tongue, and two lips?[40]

If God is compassionate and just and creates with perfection, then why is there disability? Here it is important to distinguish between the aspects of disability that involve natural evil and moral evil. In the cases that involve natural evil, we engage with the views of three theological schools: the Mutazilites, Asharites, and Maturidies.

For the Mutazilites, God is just and does not do anything unjust. He creates what benefits people. There is nothing unnecessary in his creation. If God's creation involves disability, then it is there for people to learn from. God's justice also requires an eternal reward for the people who are disabled as a result of natural evil. For the Asharites, however, God is free in his creation and creates people the way he wants. He is not obliged to create according to people's benefit. God will reward people with disabilities not because he is required to do so but because of his power, compassion, and generosity. The third school, the Maturidies, emphasize God's wisdom in creation including disability. Even if we cannot understand this wisdom, it does not mean that there is no plan behind God's creation of disability.[41]

The disabilities that involve moral evil can be discussed in the context of predestination and free will. For the Jabriya school, human movements are predestined, and therefore humans do not have power over what they do. For followers of this school, God is the sole creator, and everything depends on him. So he is the architect of all types of disabilities as the result of both natural and moral evil.

---

[39] Qur'an 32:9.

[40] Qur'an 90:8–9.

[41] Harun Isik, "Engellilik Sorununa Kelami Bir Yaklaşım," in *Ekev Akademi Dergisi* 57 (2013): 1–22.

PART III CONTEMPORARY QUESTIONS

For the Mutazilite school, people are the originators of disabilities that involve moral evil. God is just, and disabilities because of human agency are incompatible with his justice. Moral evil is the result of the freedom that humans enjoy. Those who bring about disability will face severe punishment, and those who suffer at the hands of evil people will be rewarded.

Unlike the Mutazilites, the Asharites and Maturidies believe that God is the creator of the events that involve moral evil. In this regard, God is the maker of all kinds of disabilities. However, humans will still be held accountable for their actions leading to disability. They explain this view with the doctrine of acquisition (*kasb*), because people made moral evil as their choice through their free will. While humans are not the creators of their actions causing disability, if they desire or wish to cause disability, then God creates the conditions for them.[42]

Spiritual and Practical Responses to Disability

Islamic tradition not only engages with disability theologically; it has also developed spiritual and practical approaches. First, one of the key responses to disability is patience. In a hadith, it is reported that God said that when he tests his beloved servants with blindness and they respond with patience, he rewards them with heaven.[43] Second, disability is a test not only for people with disabilities but also for temporarily abled people. It is a reminder for them to be thankful for what God has given them. Third, people with disabilities are often discussed in the context of the "needy." Muslims are encouraged to be compassionate, charitable, and accommodating toward them. Among the charitable acts listed by the Prophet

---

[42] Çağlar Tekkanat, "Bir Kelam Problemi Olarak Engellilik" (MA Thesis, Istanbul 29 Mayis Üniversitesi, 2019), 111–12.

[43] *Sahih al-Bukhari: kitab al-marda, bab fadl man dhahaba basaruhu.*

Muhammad are removing harmful obstacles that might be in one's way, helping those who have speech impediments express themselves, leading blind people on their path, and offering help to those who are in need of it.[44] Fourth, people with disabilities should have the space to participate in all matters of life, including spirituality. For example, blind people served as muezzins and *huffaz al-Qur'an* (those who know the entire Qur'an by heart) in Muslim societies. Some of them became celebrities because of their beautiful voices as well as their ability to memorize the scripture. In many cases, they would learn the Qur'an alongside sighted Muslims at the Qur'an schools. In rituals that involved the recitation of the Qur'an in people's homes, the blind *huffaz* were favored by women who preferred gender segregation. This way, the women would be out of the sight of men. One example is Shaykh Muhammad Rifat (d. 1950) of Egypt. He memorized the Qur'an by the age of ten and became one of the most gifted Qur'an reciters.[45] He was the first *hafiz* to recite the Qur'an on Egyptian Cairo radio in 1934. Rifat served as the official reciter of the Qur'an at Mustapha Pasha Mosque in Cairo for twenty-five years. Fifth, while people with disabilities will be compensated in the hereafter for their struggles and sufferings in this world, people who treat them with dignity and respect will be rewarded for their actions.

Despite the stigma toward people with disabilities in Muslim societies, disability is not regarded as a punishment or a sign of sinfulness in Islamic theology.[46] The sacred sources of Islam, including the Qur'an, hadiths, and sharia books, discuss the situation of people with disabilities and create a vision for a positive attitude in society toward them.[47] In forming a collective identity, people with disabilities have been included and remain active participants in the Muslim community

---

[44] *Hadislerle Islam*, 4:265.

[45] M. A. S. Abdel Haleem, "The Blind and the Qur'an," *Journal of Qur'anic Studies* 3:2 (2001): 123–24.

[46] Rispler-Chaim, *Disability in Islamic Law*, 11.

[47] Ghaly, "Disability in the Islamic Tradition," 158.

PART III CONTEMPORARY QUESTIONS

from the inception of Islam. The Islamic tradition emphasizes the weakness and vulnerability of all human beings in relation to God's power, so the idea of "temporarily abled people" fits into Islamic theology. It is a reminder that life is fragile and temporary. This approach can potentially form an environment where people are more mindful of people with disabilities and their dignity and become part of the effort to build a more accommodating space for them.

9 | The Environment and Climate Change

The well-being of humans and other species, including animals and plants, depends on a healthy environment. However, our planet is experiencing an alarming environmental crisis because of a number of threats, including climate change, deforestation, pollution, loss of biodiversity, oceanic dead zones, overfishing, and waste disposal. All these risks are interconnected, and they already have a significant impact on the living species, weather, and natural resources of the earth. Air pollution, for example, is considered the largest environmental health threat, causing seven million deaths every year around the world.[1] Pollution because of waste disposal can lead to increased water and marine contamination. Plastic debris can damage the soil's health and composition. It is nonbiodegradable and can stay in the soil for thousands of years, if not forever.

Global authorities have been alarmed by climate change as well. Humans have accelerated the pace of warming because of their activities such as burning fossil fuels (e.g., coal and oil), cutting down forests, and farming livestock. This has dramatically increased the amount of greenhouse gases in the atmosphere. Human-produced greenhouse gases (e.g., carbon dioxide, methane, and nitrous oxide) remain the leading causes of global warming. Because of these gases, heat that radiates from earth toward space is trapped in the atmosphere, which leads to climate change.[2] The

---

[1] "Air Pollution and Health," UNECE, accessed February 10, 2021, https://unece.org/air-pollution-and-health.

[2] "The Causes of Climate Change," NASA, accessed February 5, 2022, https://climate.nasa.gov/causes/.

PART III CONTEMPORARY QUESTIONS

decade 2010–20 was recorded as the warmest in history. The global average temperature increased by 1.1°C in 2019. Global warming because of human activities is currently increasing at a rate of 0.2°C per decade. An increase of 2°C will have devastating effects on the climate, the natural environment, and human health. That is why the international community has recognized the need to limit warming well below 2°C, preferably 1.5°C.[3] The world is already experiencing some of the consequences of climate change, such as prolonged heat waves, wildfires, droughts, floods, stronger storms and hurricanes, decreases in crop yields, loss of wildlife species, and increases in sea level.

Many major religions make a connection between the natural environment and divinity, and Islam is no exception. In this chapter, I discuss the natural world in relation to God and attempt to develop an Islamic ecological theology as a response to the environmental crisis. I begin with the natural world as a revealed sacred book.

The Natural World as a Revealed Sacred Book

The tradition of viewing the natural world as a sacred book is rooted in the Qur'an. It repeatedly draws the attention of believers to the beauties of the universe. In the scripture, for example, God swears by the olive, fig, stars, mountains, sky, and sun as the signs of God's creation.

One of the most frequently used words in the Qur'an is *aya* (sign; pl. *ayat*). As the verses of the Qur'an are referred to as *ayat*, likewise the creation is also called *ayat*. For this reason, some scholars refer to the creation as a scripture that should be read and contemplated. The creation is regarded as the expanded Qur'an of the world, and

---

[3] "The Paris Agreement," United Nations Climate Change, accessed February 5, 2022, https://unfccc.int/process-and-meetings/the-paris-agreement/the-paris-agreement.

THE ENVIRONMENT AND CLIMATE CHANGE

the scriptural Qur'an is its translation.[4] The natural world is a form of revelation.[5] The Qur'an is sacred, and Muslim scholars often discuss the etiquette of approaching the revealed text and provide a number of criteria for a proper engagement with it. Because of their respect for it, Muslims not only read the Qur'an and embody its messages in their lives; they also elevate the scripture whenever there is a chance – for example, by placing their copy on a high shelf. In addition, before reciting from the Qur'an, Muslims usually perform minor ablutions, physically purifying themselves with water.[6] Like their approach to the Qur'an, Muslims can look at the natural world in the same vein. Every single creature is a part of the pages of this book. They are sacred and should be valued like the verses of the Qur'an.

The Qur'an persistently invites believers to contemplate the natural world in relation to God:

Indeed, there are signs in the creation of the heavens and the earth, and in the alternation of the night and the day for the people of understanding, who remember God standing, sitting, and lying upon their sides, who reflect on the creation of the heavens and the earth: "Our Lord! You have not created all this in vain. Glory be to You! Protect us from the punishment of the Fire."[7]

This passage indicates that everything that is created in the universe is a "verse" of God. People should contemplate creation as such. In fact, this aspect of the natural world is also emphasized by Muhammad. According to a hadith narrated by his wife Aisha, a pair of visitors asked her to tell them something very important about the Prophet. Aisha told them that one night when the

---

[4] Nursi, *Sözler*, 224; and Nursi, *Şualar*, 922.

[5] Said Nursi, *İlk Dönem Eserleri* (Istanbul: Söz, 2009), 59.

[6] For the etiquette of approaching the Qur'an, see al-Ghazali, *Ihya' 'Ulum al-Din* (Cairo: Al-Quds, 2012), 1:450–77.

[7] Qur'an 3:190–91.

PART III CONTEMPORARY QUESTIONS

Prophet got up, made ablution (*wudu*), and performed his prayers, she saw him weeping. Tears were falling upon his beard, and his rug had become wet. Bilal, the companion of the Prophet, came for the morning prayers. He asked the Prophet: "Since all of your future and past sins are forgiven, what makes you cry?" The Prophet responded that a revelation came down the previous night, and its message caused him to weep. It would be a great shame, the Prophet said, if one were to recite it yet not engage in contemplation. The Prophet was referring to the verses cited previously. It is reported in another tradition that the Prophet said: "An hour of contemplating the creation of God (*tafakkur*) is better than one year of worship."[8] Humans are to contemplate the pages and verses of the revealed natural world.

In another verse, the Qur'an points out that everything in the universe glorifies God. There is not a single thing that does not celebrate God, although people do not understand this way of worship.[9] Because of this Qur'anic approach to the creation, some commentators indicate that "one should never show disrespect to any animal, or indeed any creature, for they too are possessed of spirit and praise."[10]

The Natural World as the Manifestation of the Divine Names

The natural world is not only a sacred book of revelation; it is also the manifestation of God's names (*asma al-husna*). Here we examine just three names. First, God is called the Pure One (al-Quddus). The Arabic root of the name (*q-d-s*) has the connotation of being pure, clean, and holy – away from impurity and imperfection. The ecological system in the natural world is the manifestation of

---

[8] al-Ghazali, *Ihya' 'Ulum al-Din* (Cairo: Al-Quds, 2012), 4:651.
[9] Qur'an 17:44.
[10] Dakake, "Commentary on *Surat al-Isra'*," 707.

THE ENVIRONMENT AND CLIMATE CHANGE

this name of God. Nursi, for example, points out that without the appearance of this name of the Creator, the scene from the natural world would look as follows:

> The corpses of a hundred thousand animal species and the debris of two hundred thousand plant species each year on the face of the earth resulting from the alternation and struggles of life and death would have so utterly contaminated the land and the sea that conscious creatures, rather than loving and delighting in the face of the earth, would have felt disgust and aversion at such ugliness and fled to death and non-existence.[11]

Humans, then, should not only reflect on the manifestation of this name of God in the natural world; they should also strive to preserve and embody it in their lives. One way to do this is to revere and protect the ecosystem of God. Humans must avoid actions that can harm the environment. This way, people will also attract God's love. The Prophet said that cleanliness is half of faith.[12] The Qur'an points out that God loves those who keep themselves pure and clean.[13]

Second, God is called the Preserver (al-Hafiz). The word in classical Arabic means "to protect, guard, take care of, and retain." One of the ways of witnessing the manifestation of al-Hafiz is to look at the seeds of trees, flowers, and plants.[14] They find life in the spring season. The safety and security of beings are the manifestations of this divine name. The Qur'an stresses that God is the guardian over everything.[15] Humans can embody this name by acting responsibly in the natural world and protecting all its creatures. Preserving life is also one of the objectives of Islamic law. Sharia not only forbids killing, including suicide, but also prohibits harmful acts toward fellow humans,

---

[11] Nursi, *Flashes*, 393.
[12] *Sahih Muslim: kitab al-taharah, bab fadl al-wudu'.*
[13] Qur'an 2:222.
[14] Nursi, *Flashes*, 188.
[15] Qur'an 34:21.

PART III CONTEMPORARY QUESTIONS

animals, and even plants. It aims to create a safe space for people to live with dignity and in harmony. For violators of this principle, sharia ensures punishment in this world as well as in the hereafter.

Third, God is known as the Just (al-ʿAdl). The root of the word is rendered as "to act justly, fairly, keep things in balance, and make things equal." The balance of the ecological system in the natural world is the manifestation of this name. All the species in the natural world are related to one another with a fine equilibrium and measure that demonstrate the manifestation of God's name the Just. Humans aim to embody this name by preserving this system. They should be just and frugal in their relations with the natural world. People should not be wasteful of the world's resources, as they will violate the rights of future generations and become objects of anger and disgust for all beings in the universe.[16] They will be held accountable for their actions on earth. The Qur'an points out that on the day of judgment, the earth will recount everything about what humans did on its surface.[17] They will be shocked by and made to cry from the accounts of the earth.[18]

Vicegerency as Responsibility

The Qur'an mentions that God created humans as the *khalifah* on the earth, which is often rendered as vicegerent, successor, or steward.[19] Despite their weakness and vulnerability, humans are privileged in the universe. However, this advantage is not about superiority and the freedom to exploit the natural world; rather, it is about their accountability. In fact, when God offered this designation to other beings such as the heavens, the earth, and the mountains, they

[16] Nursi, *Flashes*, 399.
[17] Qur'an 99:4.
[18] Qur'an 99:3.
[19] Qur'an 2:30.

THE ENVIRONMENT AND CLIMATE CHANGE

declined it because it required too much responsibility, and not fulfilling it would have consequences.[20] The Qur'an also mentions that
humans are often ignorant of the enormity of their obligation.

Muhammad pointed to the vicegerency of humans in relation to
the natural world. In one of the hadiths, he said:

> The Earth is green and beautiful. God has appointed humans as
> His stewards over it. The whole earth has been created as a place
> of worship, pure and clean. Whoever plants a tree and diligently
> looks after it until it matures and bears fruit is rewarded. If a Muslim
> plants a tree or sows a field and humans and beasts and birds eat
> from it, this is a charitable act.[21]

Here the Prophet indicates that as part of their stewardship of the
earth, humans should aim to preserve the ecosystem. The natural
world was created as clean, green, and beautiful. People should
preserve it as such, and God will reward their efforts. Based on
these Qur'anic and prophetic approaches, hunting for fun has been
mainly impermissible in Islamic law. The natural world should
even be preserved during armed conflicts. Islamic law, for example, "prohibits poisoning water supplies, destroying crops, cutting
down trees, and demolishing beehives because of the vital role food
and water play for all sources of life" in times of war.[22]

Environmental Virtue Ethics

Islamic environmental virtue ethics is another area in which to
address the environmental crisis. In what follows, I discuss some of
the virtues that can be used to tackle the problem.

---

[20] Qur'an 33:73; Qur'an 33:72; Joseph E. B. Lumbard, "Commentary on *Surat al-Ahzab*,"
in Nasr et al., *Study Quran*, 1040.

[21] *Sahih al-Bukhari: kitab al-mazara'a, bab fadl al-zar' wa al-gharsh idha 'ukila minhu.*

[22] John L. Esposito and Natana J. DeLong-Bas, *Shariah: What Everyone Needs to Know*
(Oxford: Oxford University Press, 2018), 264.

PART III CONTEMPORARY QUESTIONS

Frugality (*iqtisad*): One of the most recited passages related to frugality is in the seventh chapter of the Qur'an – "Eat and drink, but do not waste." The same verse then concludes that God does not like those who are wasteful.[23] Frugality is considered a form of thankfulness (*shukr*) in Islamic literature.[24] The continuity of the grace and blessings including the natural resources are related to being thankful to God.[25] The opposite of frugality is extravagance. The Prophet taught his followers not to be wasteful even when they did their ritual washing (*wudu*) before the prayer. On one occasion, he saw that one of his companions was using more water for his washing ritual than was needed. The Prophet asked him, "Why are you being wasteful?" The companion responded, "Is there a waste in ablution?" The Prophet then said, "Yes, even if you are making your ablution from a river you should not be wasteful."[26] Consumerism and greed can be driving forces for wastefulness. The teaching of Islam encourages believers to be content and seek simplicity in their lives. The best example for Muslims is Muhammad. He was remarkably frugal and avoided luxuries. The Prophet lived in a modest house and would sleep on a straw mat that would leave marks on his body. He would eat very little and frequently have only dates and water as his meal. Muhammad would often fast in addition to the month of Ramadan. In one of the traditions, he said: "Humans cannot fill a vessel worse than their stomach, as it is enough for them to take a few bites to straighten their back. But if they want to eat more, they then should leave one-third of their stomach for food, one-third for drink, and one-third should remain empty to breathe."[27] He only had two pairs of clothing and would

---

[23] Qur'an 7:31.
[24] Nursi, *Lem'alar*, 239.
[25] Qur'an 14:7.
[26] *Sunan Ibn Majah: kitab al-tahara, bab ma ja'a fi al-qasd fi al-wudu' wa karahiyah al-ta'addi fihi.*
[27] *Sunan Ibn Majah: kitab al-'ad'amah, bab al-iqtisad fi al-'akl wa al-karahiyah al-shiba'.*

164

THE ENVIRONMENT AND CLIMATE CHANGE

repair them when needed. Muhammad also encouraged his followers to live a frugal life, as it is considered part of the faith (*iman*).[28]

Humility: Being humble and dealing with everything in the universe with kindness and respect is one of the key teachings of Islam. The opposite of this virtue is arrogance. The Qur'an mentions that humans should not walk on the earth arrogantly. They can neither tear the earth apart nor match the mountains in height.[29] This verse is a reminder that humans should not regard themselves as superior to other creatures. The fact that so many things are in service to humans does not mean that humankind is greater than other beings; it points to their weakness and dependence. Recognizing this aspect of human nature is a means of receiving God's mercy and grace.

The Qur'an points out that living creatures are communities like human beings: "There is no animal that walks on the earth, nor bird that flies with its wings, but that they are communities like you. We have left out nothing in the Book, then to their Lord they will be gathered."[30] In other places, the Qur'an reminds readers that God revealed knowledge to the bees, and it is because of this revelation that they know how to make honey.[31] In a number of passages, the scripture indicates that there is nothing in heaven or on the earth that does not glorify God.[32] The mountains and the birds, among other creatures, sing God's praise along with the prophet David.[33] The implication of these verses is that all the beings on earth are part of the community of God, they are sacred, and they have rights independent of humans. Nonhuman creatures have a conscious relationship with God as well. Therefore, they should enjoy "the right to ethical treatment and consideration" alongside humans.

---

[28] *Sunan Ibn Majah: kitab al-zuhd, bab man yu'bahu lahu.*

[29] Qur'an 17:37.

[30] Qur'an 6:38.

[31] Qur'an 16:68–69.

[32] Qur'an 17:44; 24:41.

[33] Qur'an 38:18–19.

PART III CONTEMPORARY QUESTIONS

People should be humble and "must consider what right they have to treat God's creatures cruelly or without regard for their innate spiritual value or to utterly destroy them by using or consuming them rapaciously, irresponsibly, or wastefully."[34]

Compassion: God's mercy and compassion infuse the natural world.[35] The Qur'an repeatedly refers to God as the Most Compassionate (al-Rahman) and the Most Merciful (al-Rahim). In a number of hadiths, the Prophet encouraged his followers to be compassionate toward the creation: "If you are merciful, God is merciful to you too. Have mercy on the creatures on the earth, so those in heaven have mercy on you too."[36] In another hadith, he said: "Whoever is merciful even to a sparrow, God will be merciful to him on the Day of Judgment." Another hadith reads: "A good deed done to an animal is like a good deed done to a human being, while an act of cruelty to an animal is as bad as cruelty to a human being." One of the companions of the Prophet asked him if there would be any reward for those who would serve animals. Muhammad replied, "There is reward for serving any living being."[37] A conversation between Nursi and one of his students captures the Islamic teaching of compassion toward the natural world. On one occasion, Nursi learned that one of his students killed a lizard. Nursi was very saddened and told the student that he had committed a grievous mistake. Nursi then sat the student down for a serious lesson:

NURSI: Did the lizard attack you?
THE STUDENT: No, it did not.
NURSI: Did it grab anything from you?
THE STUDENT: No, it did not.
NURSI: Did it occupy your own land?

---

[34] Maria Massi Dakake, "Commentary on *Surat al-An'am*," in Nasr et al., *Study Quran*, 352–53.
[35] Qur'an 30:50.
[36] *Jami' al-Tirmidhi: kitab al-birr wa al-salah, bab ma ja'a fi rahma al-muslimin.*
[37] *Sahih al-Bukhari: kitab al-masaqah, bab fadl saqi al-ma'.*

THE ENVIRONMENT AND CLIMATE CHANGE

THE STUDENT: No, it did not.

NURSI: Are you the one who provides food for this animal?

THE STUDENT: No, I am not.

NURSI: Did you create this animal?

THE STUDENT: No, I did not.

NURSI: Do you know the purpose and wisdom behind the creation of these animals?

THE STUDENT: No, I do not know.

NURSI: Did God create this animal so that you kill it?

THE STUDENT: No, I do not think so.

NURSI: Then who told you to kill this animal? The wisdom behind the creation of such animals is boundless. Indeed, you committed a grave mistake.[38]

With these questions and conclusions, Nursi wanted to teach that there is no justification for harming animals. They should be handled with respect and compassion.

Eco-jihad: Jihad is one of the most important teachings of Islam. Today, the term "jihad" is almost always reduced to a fixed meaning in popular literature and often used synonymously with "holy war" or "armed combat." While seeing jihad as a fight on the path toward God became a dominant approach in some Muslim societies, the concept of jihad has always had larger implications. In reality, it encompasses an entire way of life – living in a way that is pleasing to God. Meeting this goal requires struggle and submission. Following the teachings of the Qur'an and the Sunna of the Prophet Muhammad is jihad. Following through with the five daily prayers may be an important jihad for a believer, as it is not easy to do the prayers in a modern environment with so many distractions. Giving to charity might be another form of jihad. For a social worker, taking care of the needy is a form of jihad. The jihad of a firefighter is to save lives. For a student, seeking knowledge is a jihad. According to a hadith, the

---

[38] Ahmet Akgündüz, *Arşiv Belgeleri Işığında Bediuzzaman Said Nursi ve İlmi Kişiliği* (Istanbul: OSAV, 2013), 2:518.

PART III CONTEMPORARY QUESTIONS

Prophet said: "On the day of resurrection, the ink of scholars will be compared with the blood of the martyrs on the scales, and the former will prove to be higher in status."[39] Fighting the ego is considered the greatest jihad.[40] It is believed that there is a spiritual reward for all types of jihad. This key teaching of Islam can be utilized to deal with the environmental crisis. Efforts to address this question can be considered as eco-jihad. In this regard, recycling is jihad, avoiding the exploitation of natural resources is jihad, and overcoming one's selfish desires and unnecessary consumption is jihad.

Some Initiatives in the Muslim World and the United States

Muslims around the world are making some progress toward putting the teachings of Islam into practice concerning taking care of the environment. For example, the Cambridge Central Mosque, which opened its doors to worshipers in 2019, made major news headlines as the first fully sustainable eco-mosque in Europe with a zero-carbon footprint. The project was spearheaded by two major British Muslims, Yusuf Islam (better known as Cat Stevens) and Timothy Winter, a lecturer in Islamic studies at the University of Cambridge. Concerning the project, Winter remarked, "Islamic civilization has been based on the rejection of waste as an underestimation of God's blessing, and so in the construction of the new mosque here in Cambridge, we were very much at the forefront of the local environmental movement."[41]

Because mosques are important centers of social life in Muslim societies, they can set the tone for works on environmental protection. The Moroccan government, for example, initiated a Green Mosque Project in 2015. Collaborating with the German

---

[39] Quoted in al-Ghazali, *Ihyā' 'Ulūm al-Dīn*, 1:19; and Nursi, *Lem'alar*, 278.

[40] Ernst, *Sufism*, 104.

[41] Quoted in "The Mosque," Cambridge Central Mosque, accessed February 3, 2022, https://cambridgecentralmosque.org/the-mosque/.

168

Federal Ministry for Economic Cooperation and Development, they upgraded around 900 mosques for energy efficiency by 2021.[42] The upgrades included LED lighting, solar thermal water heaters, and photovoltaic systems.

Another interesting initiative came from a group of higher education students in Abu Dhabi. Their project is called the "water-saving mosque initiative." As part of the practice of the five daily prayers, Muslims have a washing ritual (*wudu*). One Muslim believer can consume up to nine gallons of water a day. A usual mosque can potentially use up to a few million gallons of water annually. The project aims to separate and repurpose the water that is used for the washing rituals in the mosques. By using this green washing method, mosques around the world can save this resource.

Muslims in the United States have also tried to be creative in dealing with the environmental crisis. Because of the possibility of overeating during the breaking of the fast (*iftar*) and generating excessive waste during the month of Ramadan, many Muslim organizations in the United States make efforts to educate the community about having a "green" Ramadan. The motto of one such organization, aptly named Green Ramadan, is "Green your Ramadan with zero-trash *iftar* kits."[43] The same organization has also campaigned for a meatless Ramadan.[44] An Islamic organization in Chicago issued guidelines for the community during Ramadan to share food with one's neighbor, not waste food or water, plant trees, recycle materials such as plastic, and not use Styrofoam cups and plates. Ramadan sermons also urge the community to care for the environment, use energy-saving light bulbs, organize

---

[42] "Green Mosques and Buildings," GIZ, accessed February 4, 2022, www.giz.de/en/worldwide/32825.html.

[43] "About," Green Ramadan, accessed April 18, 2020, http://greenramadan.com/about/.

[44] "#MeatLessRamadan with Nana Firman," Green Ramadan, May 15, 2018, http://greenramadan.com/tag/meatless/.

PART III CONTEMPORARY QUESTIONS

mosque cleanup days, and post signs around the mosque to "go green" for Ramadan.[45]

Many Muslim-majority countries, including Bangladesh, Indonesia, and Sudan, are impacted by climate change the most. Unfortunately, some Muslim-majority countries are also known to be the most polluting states. Qatar, Kuwait, the United Arab Emirates, and Bahrain, for example, remain on the list of the top-ten countries producing carbon dioxide emissions in the world.[46] Religion is still one of the most important phenomena in Muslim societies. Islamic ecological theology can contribute much to the discourse on the environmental crisis because it teaches that the entire creation is the sacred revelation of God. The creation should be loved, revered, and read like the scriptural Qur'an. The heart of the Islamic view of the natural world is eloquently articulated by Saadi Shirazi (d. 1291). I end this chapter with his words:

> I am joyous in the world of nature
> For the world of nature is joyous through Him,
> I am in love with the whole cosmos
> For the whole cosmos comes from Him.[47]

---

[45] See Abdullah Mitchell, "Go Green This Ramadan," Council of Islamic Organizations of Greater Chicago, March 31, 2017, www.ciogc.org/5-31-17-go-green-this-ramadan-2/.

[46] "Global Historical Emissions," ClimateWatch, accessed February 12, 2022, www.climatewatchdata.org/ghg-emissions?calculation=PER_CAPITA&end_year=2018&gases=co2&start_year=1990.

[47] Quoted in S. H. Nasr, *The Need for a Sacred Science* (Albany: State University of New York Press, 1993), 129.

10 | Plagues, Pandemics, and Coronavirus

Probably nothing has caused so much suffering in a more comprehensive way than the coronavirus disease (COVID-19) in recent times. It is the manifestation of the collective pain associated with old age, sickness, and death. The pandemic hit the elderly harder than anyone. Hundreds of millions of people tested positive. Many of them got severely sick. The disease has also been one of the most deadly pandemics in history. By January 2022, almost six million people had died because of the virus – not to mention the mental illness, isolation, and unemployment that many more suffered.

While there have been diverse reactions to the pandemic, many people turned to God and religion as a response. According to one study, for example, the number of people who turned to Google searches for prayer increased significantly. More than half of the global population sought divine help to end the pandemic in the early months of the virus in 2020.[1]

Many people also emphasized the role of God in the pandemic. According to a poll conducted in 2020, more than two-thirds of religious Americans believe that the pandemic was sent by God as a warning to humans. One in ten stated that the coronavirus is related to human sinfulness. More than half of those who were surveyed noted that God would protect them from the infection.[2]

---

[1] Jeanet Bentzen, "Rising Religiosity as a Global Response to COVID-19 Fear," Vox EU, June 9, 2020, https://voxeu.org/article/rising-religiosity-global-response-covid-19-fear.

[2] "How Faith Shapes Feelings about the Coronavirus Outbreak," AP-NORC at the University of Chicago, accessed February 4, 2022, https://apnorc.org/wp-content/uploads/2020/06/Divinity_COVID_report_final.pdf.

171

PART III CONTEMPORARY QUESTIONS

Congregations of various religious traditions continued to hold their religious services communally before the vaccines became available because they believed that God would shelter them from the virus. Some of these congregations became hot spots for the spread of the virus.[3]

This chapter explores Muslim approaches to plagues and pandemics in general and COVID-19 in particular. I begin with a few verses from the Qur'an to outline some of the principles of Islamic theology concerning the pandemic.

Principles from the Qur'an and Implications for Coronavirus

First, everything is in the knowledge of God. There is nothing beyond his knowledge; God knows what is concealed in hearts and what is revealed.[4] Not even a leaf falls without his knowledge.[5] Everything in the heavens and the earth belongs to God. He has control over all things.[6] Based on these principles, the pandemic is not only in the knowledge of God but also in his control.

Second, the Qur'an mentions that God tests people with "fear, hunger, [and] loss of property, lives, and crops."[7] It encourages believers to be patient in times of trial and tribulation. In another verse, the Qur'an reads: "We will test you until We know those among you who strive and those who are patient, and We will test your reactions."[8] The pandemic can potentially be a form of test for people.

---

[3] Phil Zuckerman, "Secular vs. Religious Responses to COVID-19," *Psychology Today,* June 8, 2020, www.psychologytoday.com/ca/blog/the-secular-life/202006/secular-vs-religious-responses-covid-19.

[4] Qur'an 3:29.

[5] Qur'an 6:59.

[6] Qur'an 4:126.

[7] Qur'an 2:155.

[8] Qur'an 47:31.

PLAGUES, PANDEMICS, AND CORONAVIRUS

Third, the Qur'an repeatedly reminds people of the nature of this world; that it is uncertain and impermanent.[9] All that is on earth will perish.[10] The scripture points to the temporary nature of the world as follows:

> The parable of the life of this world is like this: rain that We send down from the sky is absorbed by the plants of the earth, from which humans and animals eat. But when the earth has taken on its finest appearance, and is adorned, and its people think they have power over it, Our Command comes upon it by night or by day, and We turn it into a mown field, as if it had not flourished just the day before. This is the way We explain the revelations for those who think.[11]

If there is anything that the coronavirus disease has demonstrated, it is that nothing is certain. While people are often attached to what they have, the pandemic has shown that things are not worth being attached to. Attachment to this world is a distraction from the hereafter.

Fourth, whereas human beings are weak and vulnerable, God is all-powerful and almighty.[12] The coronavirus has revealed the weaknesses of human beings despite the progress that has been made in many areas, including medicine. The creation, including COVID-19, is the indication of God's names. The virus's power over people can be seen as the revelation of God's name the Almighty (al-Qadir). The death of thousands of people because of the pandemic can be considered as the manifestation of God's name the Bringer of Death (al-Mumit). Millions of people recovered from the virus, which can be seen as the expression of God's name the Healer (al-Shafi).

Fifth, the pandemic forced people into lockdowns. The Qur'an often refers to the spiritual progress of prophets such as Jesus,

[9] Qur'an 29:64.
[10] Qur'an 55:26.
[11] Qur'an 10:24.
[12] Qur'an 35:44.

173

PART III CONTEMPORARY QUESTIONS

Moses, and Muhammad while in seclusion from people. The Prophet Muhammad, for example, would retreat to the cave of Hira on the mountain Jabal al-Noor in Mecca and isolate himself from society for days. It was during one of his spiritual quarantines that he received his first revelation. Social isolation was part of the spiritual journeys of many Muslim saints (*awliyah*) as well. This practice is known as *'itikaf* in Islamic spiritually. Many Muslims made connections between quarantine due to the pandemic and the tradition of *'itikaf*. Some Muslims even used the term "qu'rantine," meaning that quarantine can be taken as an opportunity to engage with the Qur'an.

Sixth, trials and tribulations are times to worship God. The idea is that people should be thankful to God not only in times of prosperity but also in times of struggle. One of the best examples is the story of Job in the Qur'an. Sickness became an occasion of worship and prayer for him. Likewise, many Muslims took the challenges of the pandemic as an opportunity to demonstrate their trust in and devotion to God.

The Prophet Muhammad and Pandemics

Muslims turned not only to the Qur'an but also to the teachings of Muhammad. His sayings and approach have been widely cited and shared in discussions about the pandemic. In one of the hadiths, the Prophet said: "Do not enter a place where there is a plague, and those who live in a place where there is a plague should not leave the area."[13] Another commonly related story is attributed to the Prophet's companion Omar. According to the account, when Omar was about to enter Damascus with his army, he was told that there was a plague in the city. Omar then did not enter the place. When he was asked whether he was running away from God's predestination, he answered that he was running away from God's predestination to

---

[13] *Sahih al-Bukhari: kitab al-hil, bab bab ma yuqrahu min al-ihtiyal fi al-firar min al-ta'un.*

174

seek refuge in his predestination. He implied that escaping from the plague was part of God's will as well.

While scholars used principles from the Qur'an and the life of the Prophet in their understanding of the pandemic, a number of approaches and controversies became apparent.

Coronavirus as a Punishment from God

Many preachers implied that the pandemic might be a warning and a punishment from God. They often gave examples from the Qur'an as well as hadiths of the Prophet. The Qur'an relates the stories of the communities who sinned, committed injustices, and disobeyed God. They faced severe punishments of plagues and natural disasters. To illustrate just a few examples, while those who believed in the message of Noah were saved, those who rejected it were drowned.[14] In the case of the prophet Saleh, those who disobeyed him were caught in an earthquake.[15] Because of their wrongdoings, Pharaoh and his people were also plagued with floods, locusts, lice, frogs, and blood and were eventually drowned in the sea.[16] In one of the hadiths, Muhammad said: "When people see an oppressor but do not prevent him from doing oppression and evil, it is likely that God will punish them all together."[17]

Martyrdom and COVID-19

Another major discussion has been whether those who lost their lives because of the pandemic, including medical staff, are considered

[14] Qur'an 7:64.
[15] Qur'an 7:78.
[16] Qur'an 7:133; Qur'an 7:136.
[17] Yahya b. Sharaf al-Nawawi, *Riyad al-Salihin: kitab al-muqaddamat, bab al-'amr bilma'ruf wa nahy 'an al-munkar.*

PART III CONTEMPORARY QUESTIONS

martyrs, the highest spiritual status in Islam. For example, amid the initial global outbreak in March 2020, a story from Iran made headlines in major news outlets. According to the news, the country's highest religious authority, the leader of the Islamic Revolution, Ayatollah Ali Khamenei, had declared the Iranian medical staff who lost their lives by contracting coronavirus while treating patients in hospitals as martyrs (*shahid*), a status that can only be attained through jihad. Those who sacrificed their lives caring for the people of Iran during the pandemic would be considered equal to Iran's fallen soldiers who defended the country during wartime. Like military martyrs, the families of fallen medical staff will now receive payments and benefits.[18]

There are a number of hadiths that imply that those who die because of a pandemic can be considered martyrs. In one of them, the Prophet said: "Any servant who resides in a land afflicted by plague, remains patient and hoping for a reward from God, knowing that nothing will befall them except what God has decreed, will be given the reward of a martyr."[19]

Proper Burial and Funerals

Having proper burials and funerals in the context of the coronavirus was another controversy among Muslims. Funerals are personal in Islamic communities. The corpse is considered to be sacred, and there is a washing ritual before the burial. However, what should be the approach to someone who died because of the coronavirus? What should be the process of burial?

Many Muslim organizations issued legal opinions (fatwas) noting that the washing ritual can be avoided if the ritual endangers the lives of the people who are handling the process. The funeral prayer

[18] Nassim Karimi and Amir Vahdet, "Iran to Call Dead Medical Staff 'Martyrs' as Virus Kills 291," *AP News*, March 10, 2020, https://apnews.com/ 12c49ab6a3f3dbc19fc1fc99dc9daa58.

[19] *Sahih al-Bukhari: kitab al-tib, bab 'ajr al-sabr fi al-ta'un.*

176

can be done with two people, and those who cannot attend can do it as absentees.[20]

A more controversial issue concerning Islamic burials during the pandemic concerned the cremation of the body, which is impermissible in Islamic law. The UK government, for example, amended an emergency COVID-19 bill in March 2020 to stop the cremation of Muslim and Jewish bodies. Families of these faiths could opt for a traditional burial. In Sri Lanka, however, the government enacted a law in the early months of the pandemic making cremation mandatory for all people who died because of the coronavirus disease. This included Muslims, who make up 10 percent of the population. Because of the opposition from the local and international Muslim community, the government eventually stopped the cremation of Muslim bodies almost a year after the breakout of the pandemic.[21]

Vaccination and Permissibility

Many Muslims questioned the permissibility of the COVID-19 vaccines because some of them may contain animal ingredients such as gelatin or animal fat, small traces of ethanol, and fetal cells (the cell lining from an aborted fetus). Muslim fatwa organizations concluded that despite what they contain, vaccines are permissible, as they save lives. The protection of life is one of the most important objectives of Islamic law.[22]

---

[20] For the overview of the fatwas regarding the burial rituals, see Ahmed al-Dawoody and Oran Finegan, "COVID-19 and Islamic Burial Laws: Safeguarding Dignity of Dead," *Humanitarian Law & Policy*, April 30, 2020, https://blogs.icrc.org/law-and-policy/2020/04/30/covid-19-islamic-burial-laws/.

[21] Haaris Mahmud, "Issue of Corona Cremations: Mr. President, Please Respect the Wishes of Muslims," *Colombo Telegraph*, March 26, 2020, www.colombotelegraph.com/index .php/issue-of-corona-cremations-mr-president-please-respect-the-wishes-of-muslims/.

[22] For example, see "The Ruling on Getting the COVID-19 (Coronavirus) Vaccine," Assembly of Muslim Jurists of America, December 13, 2020, www.amjaonline.org/ fatwa/en/87763/the-ruling-on-getting-the-covid-19-coronavirus-vaccine.

PART III CONTEMPORARY QUESTIONS

Spiritual and Practical Responses: The Case of Mehmet Görmez

Many scholars and preachers responded to the pandemic to provide spiritual and practical guidelines for Muslims. One of them was Mehmet Görmez, who served as the president of the Presidency of Religious Affairs of Turkey from 2010 to 2017. He is also an academic specializing in the field of hadith. Görmez delivered a talk concerning understanding the trials and tribulations that people endured because of the coronavirus in March 2020.[23] In what follows, I engage with some of his major points.

Görmez begins his talk with a short prayer highlighting God's name the Healer (al-Shafi) and prays for God to heal all of humanity through this name. He also prays for God to bestow his mercy and compassion upon people and dispel fear and anxiety from their hearts. However, Görmez points out that there should be a methodology guiding believers to understand the pandemic. He raises a number of questions that people often ask: Is the pandemic a punishment or a mercy from God? Is it a sign (*ayah*) of the end of the world (*qiyama*)? Is it a sign of God's creation and lesson? How should one distinguish between the roles of science and religion? He attempts to answer these questions in light of the Qur'an and the life of the Prophet Muhammad.

The Role of Religion and Science

The pandemic not only is a physical health issue, Görmez indicates, but also has spiritual aspects. Science explains the problem and its causes. Philosophy encourages us to think according to reason. Religion provides meaning. It guides us to think about the visible and invisible implications of the pandemic. Religion is not indifferent to the explanations of science and philosophy because science is

---

[23] Mehmet Görmez, "Coronavirüs Özelinde Musîbetleri Okuma Usûlü," İslâm Düşünce Enstitüsü, YouTube video, posted March 20, 2020, www.youtube.com/watch?v=3a6GWYCs3Yk.

178

PLAGUES, PANDEMICS, AND CORONAVIRUS

the interpretation of God's signs (*ayat*) and creation in the universe. Reason and thinking are God's greatest gifts to humans. Religion always played a major role in addressing people's fear of death and anxiety in the midst of calamities. Like in history, we can understand the meaning of what we are going through via religion without being indifferent to science and philosophy. Before the coming of the revelation (*wahy*), people would often interpret calamities as wars among gods, their punishments, or signs of evil people.

The Pandemic as a Divine Sign versus Punishment

If we think in light of the revelation, these trials are divine signs. We cannot think of a pandemic such as COVID-19 as a punishment. Görmez supports his interpretation with a verse from the Qur'an: "If God were to punish people for what they have earned, there would not be a single creature left on the surface of the earth. But He respites them until a specified time, and when their time comes, surely God sees His servants."[24] In another verse, the Qur'an stresses the justice of God: "Your Lord is never unjust to His creatures."[25]

As many people have claimed, the pandemic is not a sign of the end of the world either. Even Muhammad did not have the knowledge of the end of the world. On one occasion, a person came to the Prophet and asked him about the end of the world. The Prophet asked: "What have you prepared for it?"[26] He also told believers that if they knew tomorrow was the end of the world, their responsibility was to plant the tree they have in their hands.[27]

Commenting on "So take a lesson, O you have insight!" from the Qur'an, Görmez indicates that the pandemic should be seen as a lesson from God.[28] Even the disaster inflicted on the prophet Noah's people

---

[24] Qur'an 35:45.

[25] Qur'an 41:46.

[26] *Sahih al-Bukhari: kitab al-adab, bab 'alamah hubb al-allah 'azz wa jall.*

[27] *Hadislerle Islam*, 7:377.

[28] Qur'an 59:2.

PART III CONTEMPORARY QUESTIONS

was not a punishment but a lesson, as pointed out in the Qur'an.[29] People will naturally have different interpretations of the pandemic. Some will say it is because of the injustices in the world; some will say it is because of the way people treat God's creation; some will say it is because of the injustices done to Muslims in China, Myanmar, Syria, Palestine, Yemen, and so on; and some will say it is the result of people forgetting their creator, violating the rights of their families, or being indifferent to the starvation in Africa. However, the pandemic should be a means of thinking about our own responsibility, which can turn the pandemic into a mercy from God. When it is read as a sign of God, then humans can reconsider their actions and their relations with one another and with their Creator. It is also incorrect to associate the pandemic with the wrongdoings of a particular group of people. The signs of the pandemic cannot be exhausted.

Listening to Medical Experts and Prayer in Action

The recommendations of medical experts should also be taken as the instructions of the religion. The safety of people is one of the major objectives of Islamic law. Rules concerning the pandemic are consistent with the teachings of the Prophet. Following the rules initiated by medical experts is part of our religious duty. The works of scientists and medical experts are sacred because finding a cure to save lives has the highest spiritual merit. In one of the hadiths, Muhammad said the best of humans are those who benefit people.

Lockdowns can be turned into blessings. While we are away from mosques, we can turn our houses into places of worship. Görmez encourages people to rely on prayer and points to this verse: "We sent messengers before you [Prophet] to many communities and afflicted their people with suffering and hardships, so that they might learn humility. When the suffering reached them from Us, why then did they not learn humility? Instead, their hearts hardened

---

[29] Qur'an 25:37.

PLAGUES, PANDEMICS, AND CORONAVIRUS

and Satan made their deeds appear good to them."[30] He also notes that the best prayer is one that is done in action. He provides a few examples:

- Landlords can waive their rents during the pandemic.
- People can extend their hands of generosity to those who are in need.
- Employers can continue to employ their employees and pay their salaries even if they are unable to come to work because of the pandemic.
- You can take care of your neighbor and run the errands for them if needed, especially those who are vulnerable.
- Because of the pandemic, you may not able to give hugs, but you can still touch the hearts of people with your actions.

Görmez finishes his talk with the prayer of Job in the Qur'an: "Remember Job, when he cried unto his Lord, 'Suffering has truly afflicted me, but you are the Most Merciful of the merciful.' We answered him, removed his suffering, and gave him back his family along with others like them, as a mercy from Us and a reminder to the worshippers."[31]

I end this chapter with Nursi's interpretation of the Qur'anic statement that God "created everything in the best way."[32] It illustrates the Islamic theological approach to evil and suffering, including plagues and pandemics. His comments are lengthy but worth quoting:

In everything, even the things which appear to be the most ugly, there is an aspect of true beauty. Yes, everything in the universe, every event, is either in itself beautiful, which is called "essential beauty," or it is beautiful in regard to its results, which is called "relative beauty." There are certain events which are apparently ugly

---

[30] Qur'an 6:42–43.
[31] Qur'an 21:83–84.
[32] Qur'an 32:7.

PART III CONTEMPORARY QUESTIONS

and confused, but beneath that apparent veil, there are most shining instances of beauty and order.

Beneath the veil of stormy rains and muddy soil in the season of spring are hidden the smiles of innumerable beautiful flowers and well-ordered plants. And behind the veils of the harsh destruction and mournful separations of autumn is the discharge from the duties of their lives of the amiable small animals, the friends of the coy flowers, so as to preserve them from the blows and torments of winter events, which are manifestations of Divine might and glory, and under the veil of which the way is paved for the new and beautiful spring.

Beneath the veil of events like storms, earthquakes, and plague, is the unfolding of numerous hidden immaterial flowers. The seeds of many potentialities which have not developed sprout and grow beautiful on account of events which are apparently ugly. As though general upheavals and universal change are all immaterial rain. But because man is both enamoured of the apparent and is self-centered, he considers only the externals and pronounces them ugly. Since he is self-centred, he reasons according to the result which looks to himself and judges it to be ugly. Whereas, if, of their aims one looks to man, thousands look to their Maker's Names.[33]

Nursi maintains that there is no event in the universe that does not have beautiful and meaningful aspects. The transitions from one season to another manifest this reality. Humans can only see the beautiful picture behind what seems to be evil if they overcome their self-centered views and look at the events of creation from the perspectives of the divine names.

---

[33] Nursi, *Words*, 241.

Conclusion

A number of years ago, I read an article about forty maps one could study to understand our world. One of them was about Nutella, a brand of chocolate spread. The map described the process and the involvement of countries to make a single jar of Nutella. It requires natural resources and ingredients from four continents. Hazelnuts come from Turkey, cocoa is produced in Nigeria, palm oil arrives from Malaysia, Brazil provides sugar, and France contributes with its vanilla flavoring. The company that makes Nutella is based in Italy and has factories in Europe, Russia, North America, South America, and Australia. The company also has a supply and distribution chain all over the world. Millions of people with diverse ethnic, religious, and cultural backgrounds are involved in the process to bring a jar of Nutella to the breakfast table.[1] Probably no one articulated this aspect of interconnectedness and dependence better than Martin Luther King Jr.:

> You get up in the morning and go to the bathroom and reach over for the sponge, and that's handed to you by a Pacific islander. You reach for a bar of soap, and that's given to you at the hands of a Frenchman. And then you go into the kitchen to drink your coffee for the morning, and that's poured into your cup by a South American. And maybe you want tea: that's poured into your cup by a Chinese. Or maybe you're desirous of having cocoa for breakfast,

---

[1] Max Fisher, "40 More Maps That Explain the World," *Washington Post*, January 13, 2014, www.washingtonpost.com/news/worldviews/wp/2014/01/13/40-more-maps-that-explain-the-world/.

CONCLUSION

and that's poured into your cup by a West African. And then you reach over for your toast, and that's given to you at the hands of an English-speaking farmer, not to mention the baker. And before you finish eating breakfast in the morning, you've depended on more than half the world. This is the way our universe is structured; this is its interrelated quality. We aren't going to have peace on Earth until we recognize this basic fact of the interrelated structure of all reality.[2]

This reality of interconnection and mutual dependence can make us more thoughtful toward one another. One can think of evil and suffering in the same context. It is a universal experience. It is a problem that makes us all equal because it is part of human nature. Evil and suffering transcend artificial borders. If an individual has not lost their consciousness, they have the ability to have empathy not only for the suffering of their fellow humans but also for other living beings in the natural world. It does not matter whether one is part of a religious or an atheist community. Understanding the problem of evil and suffering is a struggle for both sides. While in the literature the problem is seen as a dividing question, it can also connect people regardless of their view on religion. I have observed this aspect of evil and suffering among my students. While they come to class with stark views about the issue, in the end, they come to the conclusion that the reality is more complex than they thought. There is no absolute answer to the question. For example, in facing the death of a loved one, both religious and nonreligious people struggle and grieve.

However, the role of religions in offering consolation and meaning in times of grief and suffering cannot be overstated. In this context, the strength of religion has been recognized even by thoughtful atheists and agnostics. Stephen T. Asma, an American scholar of philosophy, for example, points to this characteristic of faiths as follows:

---

[2] James M. Washington, ed., *A Testament of Hope: The Essential Writings and Speeches of Martin Luther King, Jr.* (New York: HarperCollins, 1986), 254.

CONCLUSION

I'm an agnostic and a citizen of a wealthy nation, but when my own son was in the emergency room with an illness, I prayed spontaneously. I'm not naive – I don't think it did a damn thing to heal him. But when people have their backs against the wall, when they are truly helpless and hopeless, then groveling and negotiating with anything more powerful than themselves is a very human response. It is a response that will not go away, and that should not go away if it provides genuine relief for anxiety and anguish.[3]

Alain de Botton, an atheist, maintains that some practices of religions are beneficial for society and can be used by unbelievers as well. While religious traditions have the ability to provide meaning when people suffer and teach them how to be grateful even for small successes, the secular world lacks similar skills.[4] It is in this vein that one can view the Islamic theological approach to the problem of evil and suffering in relation to God with empathy, if not admiration. In a world that looks cruel, unjust, frightening, and meaningless, the tradition offers hope, clarity, and meaning to its adherents. In what follows, I highlight some of the findings of this research.

First, God as the sole sovereign over all things is one of the most important characteristics of Islamic theology. The entire creation, including what is considered evil, is the manifestation of his names (*asma al-husna*). Without this approach, it is almost impossible to understand the problem of evil and suffering. The revelation of God's names requires diversity in the universe, which includes not only natural evil but also moral evil. There is nothing outside of God's power. This view of evil is manifested in one of the phrases that are invoked daily by Muslims: "Alhamdulillah ala kulli haal" (Thanks to God under any circumstances). They praise God in both good and bad times. The Qur'an mentions that when believers are afflicted by a calamity or go through suffering, including the death

---

[3] Stephen T. Asma, *Why We Need Religion* (Oxford: Oxford University Press, 2018), 209.

[4] Alain de Botton, *Religion for Atheists: A Non-believer's Guide to the Uses of Religion* (New York: Vintage, 2013), 188.

185

CONCLUSION

of a loved one, they remember God: "We belong to God and to Him we shall return."[5] While suffering might be a threat to their material progress, it can bring about spiritual advancement.

Second, the Islamic theological framework emphasizes humanity's limitation and imperfection in relation to God. Humans are weak and vulnerable. Suffering is part of their nature. Aging, sickness, and death are signs (*ayat*) of God's creation. Because of their freedom, while humans can potentially be very good, they also have the ability to be extremely destructive. Their selfish desires and urges are usually the root causes of moral evil. They are also limited in their knowledge of God's creation, including what they regard as evil or good. The Qur'an alludes to the inadequacy of humans as follows: "It may be that you hate something while it is good for you, and it may be that you love something while it is evil for you."[6]

Third, faith in the hereafter and accountability are significant elements of the Islamic understanding of evil and suffering. Without life after death, it is problematic to argue that God is just and benevolent. There is so much injustice in the world. Bad people who commit major atrocities often leave this world without facing the consequences of their actions. There are so many good and innocent people who suffer without any apparent justification. God's justice and compassion will be fully revealed in the hereafter. Those who cause suffering and grief will be held accountable. Good people will be rewarded for their virtuous actions, and innocents will be compensated for their suffering. Also, people long for eternity and wish to be reunited with their loved ones who have died. God will respond to their request, as he is known to be the most powerful, generous, and compassionate.

Fourth, the Islamic approach to evil and suffering falls in between orthodoxy and orthopraxy. While theology is key to understanding the problem of evil, practical responses are equally emphasized, if

[5] Qur'an 2:156.
[6] Qur'an 2:216.

186

not more important. The matter should not be exhausted with theology but rather be balanced with practice. In the case of moral evil, while the tradition attempts to provide theological answers, it also encourages believers to be just in their affairs and stand for justice, to repel evil with good, and to be forgiving and compassionate toward their fellow human beings. In facing sickness, in addition to theological responses, the tradition teaches believers to be patient and rely on God. It admonishes those who are around sick people to be caring. For those who are vulnerable in old age, it teaches filial piety. Islam's emphasis on practice has parallels with John Swinton's "practical theodicy." Grounded in the Christian tradition, Swinton believes that the classical philosophical and theological approaches to the problem of evil alone are not able to address the suffering of people. Instead, there should be responses that can benefit people in the midst of suffering to maintain their relationship with the creator.[7]

Fifth, this book does not aim to solve the problem of evil and suffering. Despite the creative efforts of Muslim scholars, there is much mystery around this matter. The Islamic approach's strength is not in offering a conclusive answer to the question but in providing meaning. This is probably the most important role of religion. As Huston Smith rightly put it: "Religion is not primarily a matter of facts; it is a matter of meanings."[8]

Finally, religion still infuses almost every aspect of life in Muslim societies. One can hardly make progress without religion in areas such as the rights of people with disabilities, the environmental crisis, and the coronavirus disease. Islam's theological framework can help tackle the problems related to these cases. Followers of religious traditions, including Muslims, and those without religion can collaborate to overcome global challenges.

---

[7] John Swinton, *Raging with Compassion: Pastoral Responses to the Problem of Evil* (Grand Rapids, MI: Eerdmans, 2007), 3–4.

[8] Huston Smith, *The World's Religions* (New York: HarperOne, 1991), 10.

Bibliography

Abas, Azura. "Forgiving US Father Receives Malaysia's Compassionate Icon Award." *New Straits Times.* December 19, 2019. www.nst.com.my/news/nation/2019/12/549299/forgiving-us-father-receives-malaysias-compassionate-icon-award.

Abdel Haleem, M. A. S. "The Blind and the Qur'an." *Journal of Qur'anic Studies* 3, no. 2 (2001): 123–25.

Abdel Haleem, M. A. S. *The Qur'an: English Translation and Parallel Arabic Text.* Oxford: Oxford University Press, 2010.

Akgündüz, Ahmet. *Arşiv Belgeleri Isığında Bediuzzaman Said Nursi ve İlmi Kişiliği,* 6 vols. Istanbul: OSAV, 2013.

Ali, Yusuf. *The Meaning of the Holy Qur'an.* Beltsville, MD: Amana, 2003.

Alper, Hülya. "Maturidi'nin Mutezile eleştirisi: Tanrı en iyiyi yaratmak zorunda mıdır?" *Kelam Araştırmaları* 11, no. 1 (2013): 17–36.

Anbeek, Christa W. "Evil and the Transformation of Evil in Buddhism and Socially Engaged Buddhism." In *Probing the Depths of Evil and Good: Multireligious Views and Case Studies,* edited by Jerald D. Gort et al., 101–16. Amsterdam: Rodopi, 2007.

Asad, Muhammad. *The Message of the Qur'an.* London: The Book Foundation, 2003.

Asma, Stephen T. *Why We Need Religion.* Oxford: Oxford University Press, 2018.

Avni, İlhan. "Aslah." In *İslam Ansiklopedisi,* vol. 3, 495–96. Istanbul: TDV, 1991.

Baglieri, Susan and Shapiro, Arthur. *Disability Studies and the Inclusive Classroom: Critical Practices for Creating Least Restrictive Attitudes.* London: Routledge, 2012.

BIBLIOGRAPHY

Baquaqua, Mahommah Gardo and Moore, Samuel. *Biography of Mahommah G. Baquaqua, a Native of Zoogoo, in the Interior of Africa* [...]. Detroit: Geo. E. Pomeroy, 1854. https://docsouth.unc.edu/neh/baquaqua/summary.html.

Baran, Sedat. "Molla Sadra'da Algısal Kötülük Bağlamında Şerr Problemi." *Şarkiyat İlmi Araştırmalar Dergisi* 11, no. 1 (2019): 13–35.

Barlow, Nora, ed. *The Autobiography of Charles Darwin, 1809–1882.* New York: W. W. Norton & Company, 1993.

Barnes, Linda L. and Sered, Susan S., eds. *Religion and Healing in America.* Oxford: Oxford University Press, 2005.

Bayhaqi, Abu Bakr Ahmad al-. *Al-Sunan al-Kubra. Cited by chapter, subchapter system.*

Bebek, Adil. "Kebire." In *İslam Ansiklopedisi*, vol. 25, 163–64. Istanbul: TDV, 2022.

Becker, Ernest. *Escape from Evil.* New York: Free Press, 1985.

Becker, Ernest. *The Denial of Death.* New York: Free Press, 1997.

Beebe, James R. "Logical Problem of Evil." Internet Encyclopedia of Philosophy, accessed January 4, 2022. www.iep.utm.edu/evil-log/#H1.

Bengtsson, Staffan. "Building a Community: Disability and Identity in the Qur'an." *Scandinavian Journal of Disability Research* 20 (2018): 1. www.sjdr.se/articles/10.16993/sjdr.18/.

Bentzen, Jeanet. "Rising Religiosity as a Global Response to COVID-19 Fear." Vox EU, June 9, 2020. https://voxeu.org/article/rising-religiosity-global-response-covid-19-fear.

Berger, Peter L. *The Sacred Canopy: Elements of a Sociological Theory of Religion.* New York: Anchor Books, 1969.

Blackburn, Simon. *Think: A Compelling Introduction to Philosophy.* Oxford: Oxford University Press, 1999.

Bourke, Vernon Joseph. *The Essential Augustine.* Indianapolis: Hackett, 1974.

Bukhari, Muhammad b. 'Ismail al. *al-Adab al-Mufrad. Cited by chapter, subchapter system.*

Bukhari, Muhammad b. 'Ismail al. *Sahih al-Bukhari. Cited by chapter, subchapter system.*

Bulut, Mehmet. "Ihve-i Selase" In *İslam Ansiklopedisi*, vol. 22, 6–7. Istanbul: TDV, 2000.

Burge, Stephen. *Angels in Islam.* New York: Routledge, 2012.

BIBLIOGRAPHY

Çağrıcı, Mustafa. "Taziye." In *İslam Ansiklopedisi*, vol. 40, 202–3. Islam: TDV, 2011.

Camus, Albert. *The Plague*. Translated by Stuart Gilbert. New York: Modern Library, 1948.

Canda, Edward et al. "World Religious Views of Health and Healing." University of Kansas, Spiritual Diversity and Social Work Initiative, accessed February 1, 2022. https://spiritualdiversity.ku.edu/sites/spiritualitydiversity.drupal.ku.edu/files/docs/Health/World%20Religious%20Views%20of%20Health%20and%20Healing.pdf.

Cheung, Ching-Yuen. "The Problem of Evil in Confucianism." In *Probing the Depths of Evil and Good: Multireligious Views and Case Studies*, edited by Jerold D. Gort et al., 87–100. Amsterdam: Rodopi, 2007.

Çolak, Yaşar. *Din, Siyaset ve Mimari: Amerika Diyanet Merkezinin Tarihi*. Istanbul: Kopernik, 2021.

Coyle, J. Kevin. *Manichaeism and Its Legacy*. Leiden: Brill, 2009.

Dagli, Caner K. "Commentary on Surat al-Anfal." In *Study Quran*, edited by Nasr et al., 482–502. New York: HarperOne, 2015.

Dakake, Maria Massi. "Commentary on Surat al-Isra." In *Study Quran*, edited by Nasr et al., 691–727. New York: HarperOne, 2015.

Dakake, Maria Massi. "Commentary on Surat al-Nahl." In *Study Quran*, edited by Nasr et al., 655–92. New York: HarperOne, 2015.

Dakake, Maria Massi. "Commentary on Surat al-Nahl." In *Study Quran*, edited by Nasr et al., 653–92. New York: HarperOne, 2015.

Dakake, Maria Massi. "Commentary on Surat al-An'am." In *Study Quran*, edited by Nasr et al., 338–404. New York: HarperOne, 2015.

Dakake, Maria Massi. "Commentary on Surat al-Isra'." In *Study Quran*, edited by Nasr et al., 693–727. New York: HarperOne, 2015.

Dawkins, Richard. *The God Delusion*. New York: Mariner Books, 2008.

Dawoody, Ahmed al- and Finegan, Oran. "COVID-19 and Islamic Burial Laws: Safeguarding Dignity of Dead." *Humanitarian Law & Policy*, April 30, 2020. https://blogs.icrc.org/law-and-policy/2020/04/30/covid-19-islamic-burial-laws/.

de Botton, Alain. *Religion for Atheists: A Non-believer's Guide to the Uses of Religion*. New York: Vintage, 2013.

de Lange, Frits. *Loving Later Life: An Ethics of Aging*. Grand Rapids, MI: Eerdmans, 2015.

BIBLIOGRAPHY

Diyanet İşleri Başkanlığı. *Hadislerle Islam*, 7 vols. Istanbul: Diyanet Yayınları, 2014.

Dostoyevsky, Fyodor. *The Brothers Karamazov*. Translated by Constance Garnett. New York: Modern Library, n.d.

Draper, Paul. "Pain and Pleasure: An Evidential Problem for Theists." *Nous* 23, no. 3 (1989): 331–50.

Draper, Paul. "God, Evil, and the Nature of Light." In *Cambridge Companion to the Problem of Evil*, edited by Chad Meister and Paul K. Moser, 65–84. Cambridge: Cambridge University Press, 2017.

Dugdale, L. S. *The Lost Art of Dying: Reviving Forgotten Wisdom*. New York: HarperOne, 2020.

Efil, Şahin. "İbn Arabî'ye göre tasavvuf felsefesinde kötülük problemi ve teodise." *Felsefe Dünyası* 1, no. 53 (2011): 92–110.

Ehrman, Bart D. *God's Problem: How the Bible Fails to Answer Our Most Important Question – Why We Suffer*. New York: HarperOne, 2009.

Eltagouri, Marva. "Why This Father Hugged the Man Who Helped Kill His Son." *Washington Post*, November 10, 2017. www.washingtonpost.com/news/acts-of-faith/wp/2017/11/10/why-this-father-hugged-the-man-who-helped-kill-his-son/.

Ernst, Carl W. *Sufism: An Introduction to the Mystical Tradition of Islam*. Boston: Shambhala, 2011.

Esposito, John L. and DeLong-Bas, Natana J. *Shariah: What Everyone Needs to Know*. Oxford: Oxford University Press, 2018.

Fakhry, Majid. *An Interpretation of the Qur'an: English Translation of the Meanings*. New York: New York University Press, 2004.

Fayyumi, Saadiah ben Joseph al-. *The Book of Theodicy*. Translated by Lenn E. Goodman. New Haven, CT: Yale University Press, 1988.

Fiddes, Paul S. "Christianity, Atonement and Evil." In *Cambridge Companion to the Problem of Evil*, edited by Chad Meister and Paul K. Moser, 210–29. Cambridge: Cambridge University Press, 2017.

Fisher, Max. "40 More Maps That Explain the World." *Washington Post*, January 13, 2014. www.washingtonpost.com/news/worldviews/wp/2014/01/13/40-more-maps-that-explain-the-world/.

Ford, Liz. "Why Do Women Still Die Giving Birth?" *Guardian*, September 24, 2018. www.theguardian.com/global-development/2018/sep/24/why-do-women-still-die-giving-birth.

BIBLIOGRAPHY

Frank, David. "1 in 3 U.S. Adults Are Lonely, Survey Shows." AARP, September 26, 2018. www.aarp.org/home-family/friends-family/info-2018/loneliness-survey.html.

Gabel, Susan L. and Chander, Jagdish. "Inclusion in Indian Education." In *Disability & Politics of Education: An International Reader*, edited by Susan L. Gabel and Scot Danforth, 69–80. New York: Peter Lang, 2008.

Ghaly, Mohammed. "Disability in the Islamic Tradition." *Religion Compass* 10, no. 6 (2016): 149–62.

GhaneaBassiri, Kambiz. *A History of Islam in America*. Cambridge: Cambridge University Press, 2010.

Ghazali, Abu Hamid al-. *The Remembrance of Death and the Afterlife*. Translated by Timothy Winter. Cambridge: Islamic Texts Society, 1989.

Ghazali, Abu Hamid al-. *The Ninety-Nine Names of God*. Translated by David Burrell and Nazih Daher. Cambridge: Islamic Texts Society, 1992.

Ghazali, Abu Hamid al-. *Ihya' 'Ulum al-Din*, 5 vols. Cairo: Al-Quds, 2012.

Goodman, Lenn E. "Judaism and the Problem of Evil." In *Cambridge Companion to the Problem of Evil*, edited by Chad Meister and Paul K. Moser, 193–209. Cambridge: Cambridge University Press, 2017.

Goossensen, Anne, van Wijngaarden, Els, and Leget, Carlo. "Ready to Give Up on Life: The Lived Experience of Elderly People Who Feel Life Completed and No Longer Worth Living." *Social Science & Medicine* 138 (August 2015): 257–64. www.sciencedirect.com/science/article/pii/S0277953615002889.

Görmez, Mehmet. "Coronavirüs Özelinde Musîbetleri Okuma Usûlü." İslâm Düşünce Enstitüsü, YouTube video, posted March 20, 2020. www.youtube.com/watch?v=3a6GWYCs3Yk.

Grewal, Zareena. *Islam Is a Foreign Country: American Muslims and the Global Crisis of Authority*. New York: New York University Press, 2014.

Hajjaj, Muslim b. al-. *Sahih Muslim. Cited by chapter, subchapter system.*

Hakkı, Erzurumlu İbrahim. *Marifetname*. Kahire: 1251H/1815.

Halverson, Jeffry R. "I Left Both Christianity and Islam Behind." *Salon*, January 5, 2022. www.salon.com/2015/08/29/i_left_both_christianity_and_islam_behind_it_was_the_problem_of_evil_and_innocent_suffering_that_truly_led_me_out_of_religion/.

Hick, John. *Evil and the God of Love*. New York: Palgrave Macmillan, 2010.

BIBLIOGRAPHY

Hume, David. *Dialogues Concerning Natural Religion*, edited by Martin Bell. London: Penguin, 1991.

Ibn Kathir, Abu al-Fada'. *Tafsir al-Qur'an al-'Azim*, 8 vols, edited by Sami bin Muhammad Salamah. Riyadh: Dar tayba lilnashr wa al-tawzi', 1999.

Ibn Majah, Muhammad b. Yazid. *Sunan Ibn Majah. Cited by chapter, subchapter system.*

Inati, Shams. *The Problem of Evil: Ibn Sina's Theodicy.* New York: Global, 2000.

Isık, Harun. "Engellilik Sorununa Kelami Bir Yaklaşım." *Ekev Akademi Dergisi* 57 (2013): 1–22.

Jackson, Sherman A. *Islam and the Problem of Black Suffering.* Oxford: Oxford University Press, 2014.

Jawziyya, Ibn Qayyim al-. *al-Tibb al-Nabawi*, edited by Muhammad Fathi Abu Bakr. Cairo: al-Dar al-Misriyya al-Lubnaniyya, 1989.

Jones, William R. *Is God a White Racist? A Preamble to Black Theology.* Boston: Beacon, 1997.

Karimi, Nassim and Vahdet, Amir. "Iran to Call Dead Medical Staff 'Martyrs' as Virus Kills 291." *AP News*, March 10, 2020. https://apnews.com/12c49ab6a3f3dbc19fc1fc99dc9daa58.

Kaya, Mahmut. "Kasidetü'l Bürde." In *İslam Ansiklopedisi*, vol. 24, 568–69. Istanbul: TDV, 2001.

Keller, Nun Ha Mim. *Sea without Shore: A Manuel of the Sufi Path.* Beltsville, MD: Amana, 2011.

Khadduri, Majid. *The Islamic Conception of Justice.* Baltimore: The Johns Hopkins University Press, 1984.

Kisakürek, Necip Fazıl. *Çile.* Istanbul: Büyük Doğu Yayınları, 2014.

Layton, J. Bradley, Smith, Timothy B., and Holt-Lunstad, Julianne. "Social Relationships and Mortality Risk: A Meta-analytic Review." *PLOS Medicine* 7, no. 7 (2010): e1000316. https://doi.org/10.1371/journal.pmed.1000316.

Levin, Jeff. "Prevalence and Religious Predictors of Healing Prayer Use in the USA: Findings from the Baylor Religion Survey." *Journal of Religion and Health* 55 (2016): 1136–58.

Levmore, Saul and Nussbaum, Martha C. "What Does It Mean to Age Well? Reflections on Wrinkles, Beauty and Disgust." *ABC*, February 4, 2019. www.abc.net.au/religion/ouraging-bodies-reflections-on-wrinkles-beauty-and-disgust/10214306.

BIBLIOGRAPHY

Lumbard, Joseph E. B. "Commentary on Surat 'Abasa." In *Study Quran*, edited by Nasr et al., 1474–78. New York: HarperOne, 2015.

Lumbard, Joseph E. B. "Commentary on Surat al-Ahzab." In *Study Quran: A New Translation and Commentary*, edited by Nasr et al. New York: HarperOne, 2015.

Lumbard, Joseph E. B. "Commentary on Surat al-Dhariyat." In *Study Quran*, edited by Nasr et al., 1273–81. New York: HarperOne, 2015.

Lumbard, Joseph E. B. "Commentary on Surat al-Jinn." In *Study Quran*, edited by Nasr et al., 1426–32. New York: HarperOne, 2015.

Mackie, J. L. "Evil and Omnipotence." *Mind* 64, no. 254 (1955): 200–12.

Mahalli, Jalal al-Din al- and Suyuti, Jalal al-Din al-. *Tafsir al-Jalalayn*. Beirut: Dar al-Qalam, 1983.

Mahmud, Haaris. "Issue of Corona Cremations: Mr. President, Please Respect the Wishes of Muslims." *Colombo Telegraph*, March 26, 2020. www.colombotelegraph.com/index.php/issue-of-corona-cremations-mr-president-please-respect-the-wishes-of-muslims/.

Maimonides, Moses. *Guide for the Perplexed*. Translated by. M. Friedländer. London: Routledge, 1904.

Maimonides, Moses. "Yesodei haTorah: Chapter One." Translated by Eliyahu Touger. Chabad.org, accessed January 12, 2022. www.chabad.org/library/article_cdo/aid/904960/jewish/Yesodei-haTorah-Chapter-One.htm.

Marshal, Amy Sarah. "Early Depression Is on the Rise." *UVA Health*, May 31, 2019. https://blog.uvahealth.com/2019/05/31/elderly-depression/.

Mawlud, Imam al-. *Purification of the Heart: Signs, Symptoms and Cures of the Spiritual Diseases of the Heart*. Translated by Hamza Yusuf. Mountain View, CA: Sandala, 2012.

Meister, Chad V. "The Problem of Evil." In *Cambridge Companion to Christian Philosophical Theology*, edited by Charles Taliaferro and Chad V. Meister, 152–69. Cambridge: Cambridge University Press, 2009.

Meister, Chad V. *Evil: A Guide for the Perplexed*. New York: Bloomsbury, 2012.

Mian, Ali Altaf. "Mental Disability in Medieval Hanafi Legalism." *Islamic Studies* 51, no. 3 (2012): 247–62.

Mill, John Stuart. *Three Essays on Religion: Nature, the Utility of Religion, and Theism*. London: Longmans, Green, Reader, and Dyer, 1874.

BIBLIOGRAPHY

Mısri, Niyazi. *Divan*. Istanbul: Emniyet Kütüphanesi Mehmed Rıza ve Şürekası, 1909.

Mitchell, Abdullah. "Go Green This Ramadan." Council of Islamic Organizations of Greater Chicago, March 31, 2017. www.ciogc.org/5-31-17-go-green-this-ramadan-2/.

Motlani, Rishad Raffi. "Islam, Euthanasia and Western Christianity: Drawing on Western Christian Thinking to Develop an Expanded Western Sunni Muslim Perspective on Euthanasia." PhD diss., University of Exeter, 2011.

Munyi, Chomba Wa. "Past and Present Perceptions towards Disability: A Historical Perspective." *Disability Studies Quarterly* 32 (2012): 2, https://dsq-sds.org/article/view/3197/3068&sa=U&ved=0ahUKEwjIpcnIlub KAhULaz4KHX_YDyoQFggoMAc&usg=AFQjCNEWDZ_ojsTk oB8Q2JDebeZ2Ngp2QQ.

Nasr, Seyyed Hossein. *The Need for a Sacred Science*. Albany: State University of New York Press, 1993.

Nasr, Seyyed Hossein, Dagli, Caner K., Dakake, Maria Massi, Lumbard, Joseph E. B., and Rustom, Mohammed eds. *The Study Quran: A New Translation and Commentary*. New York: HarperOne, 2015.

Nawawi, Yahya b. Sharaf al-. *Riyad al-Salihin*. *Cited by chapter, subchapter system*.

Nietzsche, Friedrich. *On the Genealogy of Morality*. Translated by Carol Diethe. Cambridge: Cambridge University Press, 2007.

Nigosian, S. A. *The Zoroastrian Faith: Tradition and Modern Research*. Montreal: McGill–Queen's University Press, 1993.

Novak, Philip. *The World's Wisdom: Sacred Texts of the World's Religions*. New York: HarperOne, 1994.

Nugent, Annabel. "Yusuf/Cat Stevens Reveals the Near-Death Experience That Led Him to Convert to Islam." *Independent*, September 28, 2020. www.independent.co.uk/arts-entertainment/music/news/yusuf-cat-stevens-reveals-the-neardeath-experience-that-led-him-to-convert-to-islam-b672142.html.

Nursi, Said. *The Letters*. Translated by Şükran Vahide. Istanbul: Sözler, 2004.

Nursi, Said. *The Words*. Translated by Şükran Vahide. Istanbul: Sözler, 2006.

BIBLIOGRAPHY

Nursi, Said. *Flashes*. Translated by Şükran Vahide. Istanbul: Sözler, 2007.

Nursi, Said. *İlk Dönem Eserleri*. Istanbul: Söz, 2009.

Nursi, Said. *Lem'alar*. Istanbul: Söz, 2009.

Nursi, Said. *Mektubat*. Istanbul: Söz, 2009.

Nursi, Said. *Mesnev-i Nuriye*. Istanbul: Söz, 2009.

Nursi, Said. *Sözler*. Istanbul: Söz, 2009.

Nursi, Said. *Şualar*. Istanbul: Söz, 2009.

Ormsby, Eric Linn. "Two Epistles of Consolation: Al-Shahid al-Thani and Said Nursi on Theodicy." In *Theodicy and Justice in Modern Islamic Thought: The Case of Said Nursi*, edited by Ibrahim M. Abu-Rabi', 147–58. Burlington, VT: Ashgate, 2010.

Ormsby, Eric Linn. *Theodicy in Islamic Thought: The Dispute over al-Ghazali's Best of All Possible Worlds*. Princeton, NJ: Princeton University Press, 2014.

Otieno, Pauline A. "Biblical and Theological Perspectives on Disability: Implications on the Rights of Persons with Disability in Kenya." *Disability Studies Quarterly* 29 (2009): 4. https://dsq-sds.org/article/view/988/1164.

Özay, Hilal. "İslam Hukukunda Bedensel Hükümlere Tesiri Bakımından Bedensel Engel." PhD diss., Selçuk Üniversitesi, 2010.

Ozkan, Tubanur Yesilhark. *A Muslim Response to Evil: Said Nursi on the Theodicy*. Burlington, VT: Ashgate, 2015.

Pickthall, Marmaduke. *The Meaning of the Glorious Qur'an*. New York: Everyman's Library, 1992.

Plantinga, Alvin C. *God, Freedom, and Evil*. Grand Rapids, MI: William B. Eerdmans, 1977.

Qurtubi, Abu 'Abdullah Muhammad al-. *al-Jami' al-Ahkam al-Qur'an*. Beirut: Muassas al-Resalah, 2006.

Richardson, Kristina L. *Difference and Disability in the Medieval Islamic World: Blighted Bodies*. Edinburgh: Edinburgh University Press, 2014.

Rimmerman, Arie. *Disability and Community Living Policies*. Cambridge: Cambridge University Press, 2017.

Rispler-Chaim, Vardit. *Disability in Islamic Law*. Dordrecht, Netherlands: Springer, 2007.

BIBLIOGRAPHY

Ritchie, Hannah. "What Do People Die From?" Our World in Data, February 14, 2018. https://ourworldindata.org/what-does-the-world-die-from.

Ritchie, Hannah and Roser, Max. "Natural Disasters." Our World in Data, last updated November 2019. https://ourworldindata.org/natural-disasters.

Ross, Jenna. "Global Deaths: This Is How COVID-19 Compares to Other Diseases." World Economic Forum, May 16, 2020. www.weforum.org/agenda/2020/05/how-many-people-die-each-day-covid-19-coronavirus.

Roth, Philip. *Everyman*. New York: Vintage, 2007.

Rowe, William L. "The Problem of Evil and Some Varieties of Atheism." *American Philosophical Quarterly* 16, no. 4 (1979): 335–41.

Rowe, William L. "Evil and Theodicy." *Philosophical Topics* 16, no. 2 (1988).

Rumi, Jalaluddin. *Mathnawi*. Book 1–2. Translated by Reynold A. Nicholson. London: Cambridge University Press, 1926.

Rumi, Jalaluddin, *Mathnawi*. Book 4. Translated by Reynold A. Nicholson. London: Cambridge University Press, 1930.

Rumi, Jalaluddin. *Fihi Ma Fih* [in Turkish]. Translated by M. Ülker Tarıkahya. Istanbul: Milli Eğitim Basımevi, 1985.

Rumi, Jalaluddin. "On the Day of My Death." In Diwan-e Kabir. Translated by Ibrahim Gamard. Available at Dar-Al-Masnavi, accessed May 17, 2020. www.dar-al-masnavi.org/gh-0911.html.

Russell, Bertrand. *Why I Am Not a Christian: And Other Essays on Religion and Related Subjects*. New York: Simon & Schuster, 1953.

Sachiko, Murata and Chittick, William C. *Vision of Islam*. Saint Paul, MN: Paragon House, 1994.

Sayilgan, Salih. *Exploring Islam: Theology and Spiritual Practice in America*. Minneapolis, MN: Fortress Press, 2021.

Shiraz, Shaykh Mushrifuddin Sa'di. *The Gulistan*. Translated by Wheeler M. Thackston. Bethesda, MD: Ibex Publishers, 2008.

Sijistani, Abu Dawud al-. *Sunan Abi Davud. Cited by chapter, subchapter system.*

Smith, Huston. *The World's Religions*. New York: HarperOne, 1991.

Smith, Jane Idleman and Haddad, Yvonne Yazbeck. *The Islamic Understanding of Death and Resurrection*. Oxford: Oxford University Press, 2002.

BIBLIOGRAPHY

Sönmez, Vecihi. "İslam İnancinda Günah Kavramı." In *İslami Araştırmalar Dergisi*, 28, no. 1 (2017): 42–66.

Stein, Murray, ed. *Encountering Jung: Jung on Evil*. Princeton, NJ: Princeton University Press, 1996.

Sultan, Sohaib. "Accepting the Diagnosis." *Medium*, April 11, 2020. https://medium.com/@seekingilham/accepting-the-diagnosis-3685e22af2e9.

Sultan, Sohaib. "Life Lessons: Living with Cancer." *Medium*, January 9, 2021. https://medium.com/@seekingilham/life-lessons-living-with-cancer-49940fbd3754.

Swinton, John. *Raging with Compassion: Pastoral Responses to the Problem of Evil*. Grand Rapids, MI: Eerdmans, 2007.

Syed, Ronna and Nasser, Shanifa. "Toronto Police Identify Killer in Cold Case of 9 Year Old Christine Jessop." *CBS*, October 15, 2020. www.cbc.ca/news/canada/toronto/christinejessop-news-conference-1.5763673.

Tabrizi, Imam Khatib al-. *Mishkat al-Masabih. Cited by chapter, subchapter system*.

Tekkanat, Çağlar. "Bir Kelam Problemi Olarak Engellilik." MA Thesis, Istanbul 29 Mayis Üniversitesi, 2019.

Tirmidhi, Muhammad b. 'Isa al-. *Jami' al-Tirmidhi. Cited by chapter, subchapter system*.

Turner, Colin. *The Qur'an Revealed: A Critical Analysis of Said Nursi's Epistles of Light*. Berlin: Gerlach, 2013.

Vernick, Daniel. "3 Billion Animals Harmed by Australia's Fires." WWF, July 28, 2020. www.worldwildlife.org/stories/3-billion-animals-harmed-by-australia-s-fires.

Waldmeir, Patti. "Escaping Confucian Disharmony." *Financial Times*, December 13, 2011. www.ft.com/content/a4042d52-24fd-11e1-8bf9-00144feabdco.

Washington, James M., ed. *A Testament of Hope: The Essential Writings and Speeches of Martin Luther King, Jr*. New York: HarperCollins, 1986.

Weber, Max. *The Sociology of Religion*. Translated by Ephraim Fischoff. Boston: Beacon, 1993.

Wensinck, A. J. *The Muslim Creed: Its Genesis and Historical Development*. Cambridge: Cambridge University Press, 1932.

BIBLIOGRAPHY

Winter, Timothy. "Islam and the Problem of Evil." In *Cambridge Companion to the Problem of Evil*, edited by Chad Meister and Paul K. Moser, 230–48. Cambridge: Cambridge University Press, 2017.

Youde, Fu and Qiangwei, Wang. "A Comparison of Filial Piety in Ancient Judaism and Early Confucianism." Translated by Noah Lipkowitz. *Journal of Chinese Humanities* 1, no. 39 (2015): 280–312.

Zuckerman, Phil. "Secular vs. Religious Responses to COVID-19." *Psychology Today*, June 8, 2020. www.psychologytoday.com/ca/blog/the-secular-life/202006/secular-vs-religious-responses-covid-19.

Index

9/11, 3

a'mal, 86
Abbasid dynasty, 81
Abdullah bin Umm Maktum, 146
Abraham, 47, 133, 135
Abu Bakr, 62, 149
Abu Dhabi, 169
Abu Jahl, 62
Abu-Salha, Razan, 76
Abu-Salha, Yusor, 76
acquisition. *See kasb*
adab, 122
Adam, 22, 42, 102, 123
Afghanistan
  woman in, 1
aging, 8, 97. *See also* old age
  human nature, 101
  in Islamic theology, 8
  loneliness, 99
  population in the world, 98
air pollution, 157
Aisha, 116
alam, 57
Ali ibn Abi Talib, 84, 85
Allah, 36. *See also* God
American Society of Plastic
  Surgeons, 104
angels, 8, 44–50, 90
  Gabriel, 48
  nature of, 47
  role of, 48
animal suffering, 26, 64
aql, 58
arrogance, 120
articles of faith, 126

Ashari, Abu al-Hasan, 60
Asharites, 8, 62, 82
  on animal suffering, 65
  on natural evil, 59
aslah, 59–61, 71
Asma, Stephen T., 184
asma al-husna, 160. *See also* God
atheism, 1–3
Australia, 57, 183
ayat, 158, 179, 186

Bahrain, 170
Bangladesh, 170
Baquaqua, Mahommah, 125
Barakat, Deah, 76
barzakh, 138
Becker, Ernest, 136
Bible, 47, 105
Biqai, 71
black suffering, 33
Blackburn, Simon, 13
blindness, 143, 144
Brazil, 125, 183
Buddha, 17, 18, 97
Buddhism, 8, 113, 145
  aging, 17
  asceticism, 17
  on death, 17
  eightfold path, 18
  on evil and suffering, 17–19
  four noble truths, 18
  monk, 17
  sickness, 17
Burger, Peter, 16
burial, 9
Busiri, Imam, 117

200

INDEX

Cairo radio, 155
California, 55
Cambridge Central Mosque, 168
Camus, Albert, 31
Canada, 128
cancer, 56, 112
Chapel Hill, 76
Chicago, 169
children, 1
  suffering of, 63
China, 15, 100, 180
Christianity, 8, 13, 66, 77, 105, 126,
  136, 187
  on evil, 24
climate change, 157, 170
Coastal Carolina University, 2
compassion, 5, 166
Compassion Award, 36
Confucianism, 105
coronavirus, 9, 171
  and burials, 177
  and funerals, 176
  and God's names, 173
  and Islamic law, 180
  and martyrdom, 176
  and punishment, 175, 179
  and the Qur'an, 172, 173
  and science, 178
  spiritual responses to, 178
creation, 37, 43, 158
  Adam and Eve, 43
  in the Qur'an, 158
Croatia, 3

Damascus, 103
darra, 57
Darwin, Charles, 26
Dawkins, Richard, 3
day of judgment, 138
de Lange, Frits, 101
death, 4, 9, 56, 66, 68, 98
  contemplation of, 133
  as the creation of God, 130
  fear of, 4
  life after, 126
  in Muhammad's prayer, 133
  in prayer, 134

rituals of, 137
and virtues character, 135, 136
despair, 120
dhikr, 122
disability, 9, 143, 148
  in Buddhism, 145
  and children, 145
  in Christianity, 146
  definitions, 144
  in the Greek and Roman
    cultures, 145
  in Hinduism, 145
  in Islamic law, 150
  in Islamic theology, 152, 153
  in Judaism, 146
  and leadership, 150
  models of, 144
  and predestination, 153
  in the Qur'an, 146–48
  and spirituality, 154
  in the United States, 144
  in the world, 144
disease, 115
Dostoyevsky, Fyodor, 29
dua, 113, 122
Dugdale, Lydia S., 104

earthquakes, 14, 62
eco-jihad, 167
eco-mosque, 168
Egypt, 89, 117, 155
Ehrman, Bart D., 2
eid prayer, 151
environment, 9, 157
  and Islamic law, 163
  virtue ethics, 9, 163–68
envy, 120
Epicurus on evil, 24
eschatology. *See* hereafter
Europe, 183
euthanasia, 133
Eve, 22, 42, 102
evidential problem of evil, 28
evil
  definition, 14
  definitions in Islamic literature, 57
  as a test, 72

201

INDEX

fahsha, 57
famine, 90
faqr, 122
fasad, 57, 60
filial piety, 9, 100, 104, 106, 107, 109
fiqh, 7
freedom, 90, 92
funerals, 9

Gaon, Saadia, 22, 64
Garden of Eden, 22
Gautama, Siddhartha. *See* Buddhism
German Federal Ministry, 169
Ghazali, 2, 8, 44, 67, 69, 70, 121
God, 1
  attributes, 40
  and creation, 159
  and the creation natural evil, 58
  and disability, 144
  grace, 62
  as the healer, 115
  jalali and jamali names, 40–42
  justice of, 5, 9
  manifestation of, 1
  mercy, 1, 5
  names of, 38–40
  natural evil and names, 65
  nearness and distance, 40
  the source of peace, 44
  wisdom of, 60
Görmez, Mehmet, 178
grace, 110
Green Mosque Project, 168
Green Ramadan, 169

hadith, 9
  al-qudsi, 37, 42
  on God's mercy, 42
hafiz, 155
Hakkı, Erzurumlu İbrahim, 74
Halverson, Jeffry R., 2
Hanson, Hamza Yusuf, 5, 55
Harvard University, 143
hatred, 120
headscarf, 143
healing, 9, 114, 146
health, 113

heaven, 126
Hebrew Bible, 22, 113
heedlessness, 120
hell, 126
hereafter, 9, 134
  attributes of God, 128
  justice, 128, 129
  theology, 128
Hick, John, 23
hijama, 117
Hinduism, 145
Hitler, Adolf, 129
Holocaust, 33
Holy Spirit, 114
Hoover, Calvin, 129
hudud, 150
huffaz al-Qur'an, 155
human nature, 51, 53
humanism, 33, 34
humanocentric theism, 34
humans and God's names, 42, 43
Hume, David on evil, 25
humility, 165
Husayn ibn Ali, 84
Hussein, Saddam, 129
huzn, 57

ibadat, 150
Iblis. *See* Satan
Ibn al-Munayyir, 71
Ibn Arabi, 8, 70
Ibn Sina, 8, 67
Ibrahim, the Prophet's son, 131
ikhlas, 122
ikhwah al-thalathah, 60
illness, 68, 98, 116. *See also* sickness
  as God's creation, 115
  spiritual illness, 120
  and spiritual progress, 118
imam, 150
iman, 86, 165
Indonesia, 170
innocent suffering, 62–64
iqtisad, 164
Iran, 1
Ireland, 3
Irenaeus, 24

202

INDEX

Islam, Yusuf, 168. *See also* Stevens, Cat
Israeli, 3
itikaf, 174
iwad, 63

Jabriya, 80
Jacob, 89, 90
Jahm bin Safwan, 80
janaiz, 136
Jessop, Christine, 128
Jesus, 3, 23, 105, 113, 146
Jews, 3
jihad, 92, 167, 168
jihad al-nafs, 121
jinn, 8, 50
Jitmoud, Abdul Munim Sombat, 35
Jitmoud, Salahuddin, 35
Job, 113, 120, 174, 181
Joe Biden, 143
John the Baptist, 109
Jones, William R., 33
   humanocentric theism, 34
Joseph, 89, 90, 148
   and death, 134
ju, 122
Jubbai, Abu Ali, 60
Judaism, 8, 13, 77, 105, 113, 126, 146
Jung, Carl Gustav, 20
Juwayni, 2

Kaaba, 37, 138, 151
kabad, 87
kabira, 84
kasb, 8, 82
Keller, Nuh Ha Mim, 74
Kentucky, 35
khalifah, 162
Khamenei, Ayatollah Ali, 176
Kharijites, 85
khayr, 57
Khidr, 87
King Jr, Martin Luther, 183
kufr, 44
Kuwait, 170

Lennon, John, 3
logical problem of evil, 26

Mackie, J. L., 26
mahabba, 122
Maimonides, 19–20
Malaysia, 36, 183
Manichaeism, 15
marifa, 122
martyrdom, 176
Mary, 45
Masjid al-Nabawi, 148
Maturidis, 8, 61, 82
   on natural evil, 60
Mawlud, Imam Muhammad, 122
Mecca, 37, 50
   polytheism in, 126
mental illness, 14
mercy, 5
Mill, John Stuart, 25
minbar, 151
Minkara, Sara, 143
Misri, Niyazi, 111
monk, 98
monotheism, 37
moral evil, 8, 14
   and God's names, 90, 91
   and human agency, 8
   and justice, 92
   response to, 92
Morin, Guy Paul, 128
Morocco, 168
mortal sinner, 85
mortality, 112
Moses, 87, 148
mother, 1
   compassion of, 1
   sacrifice of, 1
muamalat, 150
muezzin, 148
Muhammad, 36, 56, 155, 163, 164
   death of, 131
   and disability, 149
   on diseases of the heart, 120
   on healing, 116
   on visiting the sick, 123, 124
mukhalafat al-nafs, 122
Murjiites, 85
musiba, 57
Mustapha Pasha Mosque, 155

INDEX

Mutazilites, 8, 61
  on animal suffering, 65
  on innocent suffering, 63
  on natural evil, 59
  on predestination, 81
Myanmar, 180

nafs, 52, 121, 138
natural evil, 14
natural world, 166
  and God's names, 160, 161
  in the Qur'an, 158
  and responsibility, 163
Netherlands, 100
New Testament, 45, 113, 148.
  See also Bible
New York, 125
Nietzsche, Friedrich, 32
Nigeria, 183
North America, 183
North Carolina State University, 76
Nursi, Bediuzzaman Said, 7, 8, 62, 67,
  108, 181
  and environment, 166
  on human suffering, 66

old age. *See also* aging
  in the Qur'an, 101, 102
  spirituality, 110
Omar ibn al-Khattab, 174
Ontario, 128
Ottoman language, 7

Pacific Ocean, 6
pain, 112
Palestine, 3, 180
pandemics, 9, 171
  and Muhammad, 174
patience, 120
peacock, 67
Persian, 103
physical pain, 14
plagues, 9
Plantinga, Alvin, 27, 28
Plato, 145
poetry, 7
pollution, 157

polytheism, 37
practical theodicy, 187
predestination, 8, 78, 83, 86
  Asharites, 81
  human agency, 79–84
  Jabriya, 80
  Maturidi, 81
  mortal sin, 84
  Mutazilites, 80, 81
Princeton University, 112
prison, 89
pulpit, 152

qada, 8, 78
qadar, 8, 78
qanaa, 122
qasida al-burda, 117
Qatar, 170
qiyama, 130
qudrah, 59
Qur'an, 9, 35
  creation in, 37
  forgiveness, 35
  as healing, 118
  natural evil, 58
Qurtubi, 63
Qushayri, 2, 122

repentance, 55
resurrection, 9
  in the Qur'an, 126, 127
Rifat, Shaykh Muhammad,
  155
Roman Catholic Church, 114
Roman Empire, 15
Roth, Philip, 99
Rowe, William L., 28, 29
ruh, 52, 138
Rumi, 8, 68, 72
  on death, 130
  on sickness, 119
Russell, Bertrand, 4
Russia, 183

sabr, 74, 122
sacraments, 114
sadaqa, 62

204

INDEX

Sadra, Mulla, 66, 70
salat, 123
salat al-istisqa, 56
samt, 122
Satan, 15, 28, 43, 121, 181
  and disobedience, 51
sayyia, 57
Serbia, 3
Shabbi, Abu al-Qasim, 93
shahadah, 137
shaqawa, 57
sharia, 161
sharr, 57
shawq, 122
Shiite, 7
Shirazi, Qutb al-Din, 70
Shirazi, Saadi, 170
shirk, 44
shukr, 122, 164
sickness, 9. *See also* illness
  responses to, 120
sin, 120. *See also* mortal
  sinner
Solomon, 50
South America, 183
Soviet Russia, 7
Sri Lanka, 177
Stevens, Cat, 6
su', 57
Sudan, 170
Sufism, 7, 121
suicide, 132
Sultan, Sohaib, 112
Sunna, 167
Sunni, 7, 81
Surat al-Fatiha, 138
Surat al-Yasin, 137
Suyuti, 46
Swinton, John, 187
Syria, 180

ta'ziya, 138
tafakkur, 43, 160
Taliban, 1, 3

tark al-shahwa, 122
tawadu, 122
tawakkul, 73, 122
tawba, 55, 122
tazkiyah al-nafs, 121
tibb al-nabawi, 117
Turkey, 1
Turkish language, 7
Turner, Colin, 82

Umayyad dynasty, 80
United Arab Emirates, 170
United Kingdom, 99
United States, 144, 152, 169
universe, 160
University of Cambridge, 168
University of North Carolina, 76
Uthman bin Affan, 84
uzla, 122

vaccination, 177
vicegerency, 163
visiting the sick, 123

wahy, 179
wara, 122
wasiya, 107
Weber, Max, 16
Wellesley College, 143
West Africa, 125
World War I and II, 7
wudu, 160, 164, 169

Yemen, 180

Zachariah, 45, 102, 110
Zayn al-Din Ibn 'Ali, 63
Zaytuna College, 55
Zoroastrianism, 8
  Ahura Mazda, 15
  Angra Mainyu, 15
  on evil, 15
zuhd, 122
zulm, 57

www.ingramcontent.com/pod-product-compliance
Ingram Content Group UK Ltd.
Pitfield, Milton Keynes, MK11 3LW, UK
UKHW032107190125
453804UK00006B/41